MW01233817

HYDROPONIC GARDEN SECRETS

GREENHOUSE GARDENING FOR BEGINNERS

OLIVER GREEN

© **Copyright 2021 - *Oliver Green***
All rights reserved.

This report is towards furnishing precise and reliable data concerning the point and issue secured. It was conceivable that the manufacturer was not required to do bookkeeping, legally approved, or anything else, competent administrations. If the exhortation is relevant, valid, or qualified, a rehearsed person should be requested during the call.

The Declaration of Principles, which the American Bar Association Committee and the Publishers and Associations Committee have accepted and supported.

It is not appropriate to reproduce, copy, or distribute any portion of this report in either electronic methods or in the community written. Recording this delivery is carefully disclaimed, and the ability of this report is not permitted until the distributor has written a license. All rights. All rights held.

The data provided in this document is expressed in an honest and predictable way, like any risk, in so far as abstention or anything else, is a singular and articulate duty for the beneficiary peruser to use or mistreat any approaches, procedures or bearing contained within it. No legal responsibility or blame shall be held against the distributor for any reparation, loss, or money-related misfortune because of the results, whether explicitly or implied.

All copyrights not held by the distributor are asserted by individual authors.

The details herein are solely for educational purposes and are all-inclusive. The data was entered without a contract or acknowledgment of assurance.

The marks used shall be without consent, and the distribution of the mark shall be without the consent or support of the proprietor of the mark. All trademarks and trademarks within this book are just for explanation and are held clearly by the owners, who are not associated with this record.

Table of Contents

HYDROPONIC GARDEN SECRETS

HYDROPONIC GARDEN SECRETS

A PROVEN SYSTEM FOR BEGINNERS TO GROW VEGETABLES, FRUITS AND HERBS WITHOUT SOIL FASTER WITH A SIMPLE 8 STEP FORMULA

OLIVER GREEN

Introduction

Gardening is one of the most common interests of people around the world. Everyone wishes to produce his or her own little corner of garden production. A garden can also be the source of relaxation for an individual, as well as for personal satisfaction.

Hydroponics has been the dream of gardeners for over a decade. In the 1920's, in Munich, an experimenter and horticulturist named Heinrich Dorner discovered that by placing plants in a controlled environment with their roots in water, they would grow faster and with better results than traditional gardening methods.

During World War II, this theory was tested at the University of California at Berkeley. The results were amazing; it was found that with hydroponics, a plant could be grown in the casing that only contained 10% water and everything else could be cut to reduce weight. This led to new techniques for water conservation and new methods of selecting plants for landscaping purposes.

In the 1950's, hydroponics became popularized by Dr. Luther Burbank, a horticulturist who attempted to create an entirely new breed of the plant by using new hybridization methods. During the 1960's, many more seeds were sent off to space using NASA's space program. Pots were sent up as part of the program for test runs but apparently, all perished after returning to Earth due to the different conditions they faced. However, it is rumored that one survived and is now thriving in a secret location somewhere on Earth.

Hydroponics is growing plants without soil. It's a technique that uses the power of water to nourish the roots of your plants instead of dirt. Hydroponics produces high yields, with minimal effort and fewer pests than traditional growing methods. It helps to alleviate the need for pesticides, which have adverse effects on both humans and insects. Hydroponics is having a little revival, and for good reason. It offers a lot of advantages over traditional gardening methods. Hydroponics is also becoming increasingly popular, and people are taking advantage of the way it can help them grow their plants.

It's a proven technique used by experts for decades. It doesn't require soil, pesticides, or chemical fertilizers. Instead, it relies on the water flowing through your hydroponics system. Plant roots absorb up to three times more water than they exhale and all needed nutrients are absorbed, even during dry periods. To keep your hydroponics system running smoothly, we highly recommend using nutrient-rich water. The more nutrient-rich water that your plants get, the better it will turn out. The nutrient-rich water used in hydroponics is easily recycled and can be used for other purposes, making it a sustainable alternative method to traditional gardening.

Hydroponics is becoming more popular because it is inexpensive and allows you to grow fruits and vegetables that would otherwise be difficult or impossible to grow in your home garden. Hydroponics can also be used in an office or school environment and is not limited to just fruits and vegetables. With hydroponics, you can grow cannabis indoors with a minimal amount of human intervention. There's nothing to worry about pest infestations or diseases. You also won't have to be concerned about how much sunlight your plants receive.

Hydroponics allows you to grow a wide variety of vegetables. You can even grow fruit if the right equipment is used (such as hydroponic systems that produce "grow lights" for germinating seedlings). Hydroponics allows you to create nutrient-rich pools for different types of plants, which can then be planted together in your garden. In addition to vegetables, you can also grow strawberries, pumpkins, melons, and many other common fruits.

The most common form of hydroponic garden is actually called a closed-loop system. The closed-loop system uses recycled water and nutrient solutions to grow your plants in completely sterile conditions. This ensures that your plants will not be exposed to any pathogens from the ground or from pesticides used on the plants before harvest.

There are also more modern systems that do not use recycled water or chemicals to grow your plants but use only natural resources. These systems use nutrients and light to produce the plants you desire. If you prefer something a little more hands-off, you can even use some type of automated hydroponic system that relies on computer controls and sensors to monitor plant growth. Without the need for constant attention from you, these types of systems give you much more flexibility.

CHAPTER 1.

What Is Hydroponics?

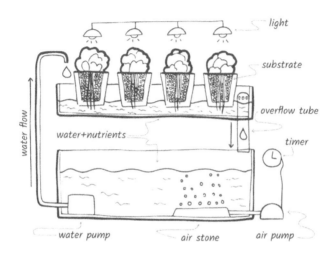

History of Hydroponics

O ur beginnings go back all the way to the 1600s. Hydroponics, or "water culture," is the oldest known form of plant cultivation. Since that time, hydroponic gardening has grown in popularity and range of application.

The original purpose of hydroponically growing plants was to supply fresh products for people who were unable to work in the fields due to a lack of irrigation or storage facilities. The invention of the hydroponic growing system made it possible for indoor growing on an industrial scale.

Since then, hydroponic gardening has expanded its applications to include environmentally-friendly gardening, as well as food production for animals and human consumption. As such, it has become a very useful tool in maintaining crop quality, increasing yield, and reducing food safety risks associated with traditional methods of agriculture.

Hydroponics is a great way for farmers to grow high-quality crops at minimal cost—there are no pesticides, no herbicides, no chemicals whatsoever. Instead, all you need are nutrient-rich water and trace elements—things like iron, magnesium, calcium, nitrates, and phosphates (salt water).

Hydroponics has become a worldwide phenomenon in the last 50 years, especially with the advancement of LED lighting. Due to the strict rules governing genetically modified organisms, hydroponic farmers have had no choice but to use non-GMO plant materials.

Gradually, new strains were created, and now farmers have access to a wide variety of organic seeds and plants. Hydroponic gardening changed the way plants are grown, and now seeds and plants are grown in completely natural environments, thanks to LED lighting.

Why is Hydroponics Interesting in Today's World?

Hydroponics is the answer to the growing concern for food production and food quality. Agricultural land worldwide is fast becoming short and that may lead to scarcity of food or insecurity of the food supply. Additionally, the productivity of farmlands is declining over time. Soil infertility is equivalent to low-quality food. The old system of rotation can only work for a certain number of years without depleting soil quality.

Through hydroponics, individuals may be assured that food is always available and that the crops are easy to harvest. Also, in areas with non-arable land, crops can be grown. Hydroponics ensures that to grow well, the plants or crops get the nutrients required.

The Growing Process of Hydroponics

The Era of Astonishment

In some parts of the world, we are still living the ordinary life, with all the necessary facilities and with the help of natural resources like in African and Asian continents. But at the same time, we are also the human species who are learning and working on the concept of artificial intelligence.

What Have We Done So Far?

In our short span of human life, we have attained all the necessary facilities of living with some magical technological and science inventions such as mobile phones for excellent communication, motor vehicles for a luxurious life, military weapons for hegemony establishment and who can forget the ongoing era of the digital world. Overall, it's a digital age and a period of technological advancement.

New Way of Plantation

Indeed, it's a new era because today we have changed all mathematics of nature by growing plants without soil. It is quite surprising and astonishing, but it's a fact now. Developing a plant without soil is known as hydroponics. So, now let's understand this term and method of plantation profoundly and figure out the growing process.

Hydroponic—What Does It Mean?

We know it's pretty confusing and astonishing enough when discussing farming and gardening without soil. Since our childhood, we have been watching the growing process of wheat and fruits through the land. And it seems like a pretty extraordinary thing. Science says, when we grow the plant roots with water and nutrient solution without soil, it is considered as a hydroponic process.

Hydroponic, the term looks like an arduous phenomenon of science and is hard to explain. But it is quite simple because the name of hydroponic says 'the growing of plants or farming without soil.' It means that with the help of nutrients and water we can grow any plant. So, let's understand this deeply.

We all have read about the growing process of plants in our school's science book. The method of making glucose from sunlight and the chemical found in plant's leaves and the overall process is called photosynthesis.

The Theory behind Hydroponics

The theory behind hydroponic says that through water, growing medium (reservoir), and nutrients we can build a plant more effectively rather than soil-based growth. In a nutshell, the sole focus behind this theory is that experts want to eradicate every possible obstacle or barrier between plant roots and water, nutrients, and anything necessary for healthy growth.

$6CO_2 + 6H_2O \rightarrow C_6H_{12}O_6 + 6O_2$ is the sole process of photosynthesis. It means how a plant grows and what kind of element and things they need in their growing stage.

The plant grows through a process called photosynthesis. In this particular process, they use a chemical that is present in their leaves called chlorophyll and sunlight to convert water and carbon dioxide, which is present in the air, to produce oxygen.

And if you have noticed that, then you can identify that the soil is not mentioned here to grow the plant. And this is one of the most significant scientific proofs about the growth process of plants without soil.

The Growing Process of Hydroponics

After discussing the chemical equations, methods, and theory behind the plant growth, now let's figure out the process of hydroponics. So, it is pretty much clear now that you need water, sunlight, and nutrients.

We use soil to obtain water and nutrients, and if we get them without ground, then there is no need for land for the plant growing process.

And that is the sole theory behind the concept of hydroponics. Hydronic means to build a plant in water and most of the people called it the growth of a plant without soil.

Why Grow Plants Hydroponically?

Hydroponic is one of the biggest questions that is roaming all around the minds of people about the hydroponic process because our generation is now used to it. From our primary education to higher education, we learn how a plant grows from the soil by doing the natural process of photosynthesis, and suddenly a new term comes and redefining all the essential learning of people.

Plant and nature experts say that there are numerous benefits of growing plants through the hydroponic process. While doing the experiment process and growth, some researchers have found some extra-beneficiary growth of the plant through the hydroponic method.

The Secret of Hydroponics Success

If you want to be successful in the hydroponic industry, then you only need skills, dedication, and must have a keen desire to grow crops. It is not necessary that the person who is going to do hydroponic gardening must have previous farming experience, but it can be very helpful in understanding things in a better way.

With limited resources and a surging population, traditional farming is on the back foot as there is a scarcity of land; that's why several growers are looking forward to hydroponic farming.

According to the latest report, it is stated that by 2050, there will be a drastic jump in the overall population that is from 7.3 to 9.8 billion. Due to this reason, there is a need for food that will surge from 58% to 98% in the coming 30 years.

Farmers are concerned with regards to this as land is not available for the crops to grow. Thanks to hydroponic farming that has allowed growing the plants. The recent trend of hydroponic agriculture has captured the minds of farmers up to a great extent; that's why they are shifting from traditional farming to the hydroponic system.

The main benefit of this farming is that it is very versatile; the system of hydroponic can be placed anywhere, etc.

CHAPTER 2.

The Advantages and Disadvantages of a Hydroponic System

Advantages of Hydroponic Gardening

Improved Genetic Health

Plants in a hydroponic system are not only provided with nutrition that has an almost perfect composition, but they are also safeguarded from many potential pests that they could otherwise come into contact with when growing in the soil. This allows the plants to reach a higher level of genetic health. As the saying goes, 'you are what you eat.'

High-scale Production

Although hydroponics can be used to create your variety of plants at home, an often-surprising fact is that the hydroponic process is responsible for providing food to millions. The science has now been enhanced to a level at which more fruit, vegetables, and herbs can be produced at a higher quality than ever before! Yields from growing hydroponically are at least 20% greater than with growing with soil.

Affordable

Hydroponics will allow you to say goodbye to the often-costly ordeals of obtaining prepared soils and plant protection products. On top of this, most of the standard gardening tools (e.g., trowels, shovels, forks) are not needed.

Less Time, More Produce

The process of planting becomes a breeze because you will no longer have to spend time preparing soil between plantings. On top of this, your plants will be able to mature faster, generating an abundance of beautiful products.

Vegetables, Fruits, and Flowers Grow Healthier

With hydroponics, plants get the right kinds of nutrients in the right amounts at the right time, which means that they contain the correct nutritional values in the product. Studies show that there is 50% more nutritive content in crops grown in hydroponic gardens in contrast to traditional ones.

Faster, Better Results Are Achieved

Since nutrients are introduced and adjusted in the water, the plants feed directly and do not expend much energy tracing and extracting the needed supply of nutrients. They grow faster, bigger, and in superior quality. In this sterile and controlled environment, you will get twice the yield from your crops.

Hydroponic Gardens are Easy to Maintain

You can have a garden without soil indoor or outdoor. You require less labor in the setup and upkeep of a hydroponic garden. You don't need to test your soil or setup a plot. You can also use commercially available pH-balanced nutrient solutions.

You Can Grow and Enjoy Your Crops

A lot of people worry about the chemical content in their food because of inorganic fertilizers, insecticides, and other plant sprays. Growing your vegetables and fruits at home can give you the peace of mind that what you are eating is fresh and free from chemicals.

In a hydroponic garden, it is easy to harvest vegetables, fruits, and flowers. Moreover, you save more money.

You Can Grow Plants Anywhere

You only need a growing medium, water system, nutrient solution, and a light source, and you're good to go. Remember that plants will grow if their needs are met.

You Save Space

Unlike in soil gardens, you cannot have plants grow too close together or they will fight each other for nutrients. In a hydroponic garden, you can place plants with small roots together, and they will grow just as big and healthy as a traditional garden.

You Help Protect the Environment

Traditional gardening leads to the degradation of soils as high amounts of potassium, phosphorus, and calcium are introduced to it through fertilizers. Hydroponics is a good way to reduce the amount of arable land.

Also, you need far less water for a hydroponic garden than you would in a soil-based one, which contributes to conserving our Earth's water.

Hydroponic Gardening is Fun and Relaxing

Hydroponic gardening is advantageous not only to commercial farmers but also to home gardeners and those who are looking for hobbies. Soil-less gardening is a fun, innovative, and a great way to relax or spend time with your family. Additionally, there is much less physical labor involved in hydroponic gardening as compared to conventional gardening. It is a great stress reliever, as well. What can be more relaxing and rewarding than seeing the fruits of your labor literally, right in your own home?

There is Little Chance of Environmental Degradation

Fertilizers are not required in hydroponic farming. Additionally, you don't need to worry about changing seasons and weather conditions. Often, bad weather leads to the destruction of prized plants, flowers, and crops that you've worked so hard to cultivate, but with a hydroponic system, you can avoid these natural disasters.

There is Very Little Wastage of Resources in Hydroponic Farming

Waste products are reduced because dirt and soil are not utilized. Water is easily disposed of in a clean and proper way. This reduces the possibility of over or under-watering. The supply of nutrient water is regulated; therefore, you will not have to double-check if the water is enough or not.

The money you invest in preparing a garden and maintaining it is returned through products that you can eat or sell for profit.

Safer and Less Need for the Use of Pesticides and Chemicals

With hydroponic gardening, you also eliminate the possibility of pest infestation, therefore also removing the use of pesticides. This leads to a much healthier garden and products.

Improved Home Environment

Hydroponic gardens are some of the most beautiful gardens to have in your home. You can drastically upgrade the look of your environment through hydroponic gardening. Just as the site of an aquarium in your house is breathtaking, so is the site of plants in your home.

The Relieved Strain on Your Budget

Food is expensive, even more so are fresh fruits and vegetables. You can make a great cut in your household budget by simply utilizing your free space by having a hydroponic garden.

Enriched Skills

A Hydroponic garden is not just a garden, but a botanical laboratory of its own kind. You get to learn a lot about plants—how to take care of them, their basic requirements, and how to maximize yields. You also learn how to utilize your farming skills as you get exercise and learn how to create a scenic, green landscape around your compound.

CHAPTER 3.

Disadvantages of Hydroponic Gardening

Cost of Setup

Many traditional hydroponic setups can be quite expensive when you buy growing tents, lighting systems, and more. Although, prices are coming down due to LED lighting systems and other advances in technology. There are affordable hydroponic systems available, though you are limited in what can be grown in these.

Space Requirements

Depending on the system you choose, it will need space indoors, perhaps in a garage or spare room. Some people will grow in their attic or basement, though if space is limited, look at the Ikea-style growing systems that can be used on a kitchen countertop.

Learning Curve

Growing in soil is relatively easy and, although there is a lot to learn, can be done without any expert knowledge. Hydroponic gardening does require some knowledge to choose the right type of lights, ensure they give out the right light spectrum at the right time, monitor the pH levels, and more.

Regular Checking

You must regularly check your hydroponic system, monitoring nutrient and pH levels. Initially, this may be quite difficult while you get used to it, but as you get used to hydroponic gardening, this will require less work. It can make vacations a little tricky, but most hydroponic systems will cope with being left alone for up to a week.

Water-based Microorganisms

However, through proper hygiene and care the chances of this is minimal, particularly as you monitor the system regularly and can spot problems before they become serious.

Limited Range of Plants

Not all plants are suitable for hydroponic systems to develop in, and depending on the method you are using, you may only be able to produce certain types of plants or only a single type of plant at a time.

Diseases Spread Rapidly

Because the plants are spaced closer together and can often be the same type, if any diseases should get into the system, then they can spread very quickly. If should a disease is introduced, you will need to sterilize your entire system and start again. However, diseases are rare in hydroponic systems when proper hygiene is practiced, and new plants enter quarantine before introduction.

CHAPTER 4.

Overview of the Different Systems and How to Build Your Own

Wick Systems

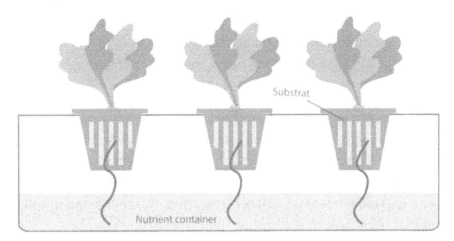

Wick systems are easy to understand and have simple components, cheap assembly, and low maintenance. Although they are part of hydroponic crops, they do not include water pumps or diffuser stones.

Since the plant controls the process, it will only absorb the liquid it needs. The wick must be long enough so that one end is submerged in the liquid mixture, and the second end is in contact with the plant's root system. An alternative crop substrate to the soil must be used. Sand, gravel, or pearlite are viable options since they can all absorb and retain moisture.

Standard hydroponic systems usually require expensive equipment and a deep understanding of cannabis cultivation. So why are wick systems so interesting? Although they still require conventional knowledge about the cultivation of marijuana, wick systems eliminate certain complications that could cause problems for novice growers.

The fact of not using land eliminates some risks such as pests, mold, and pollution. The wick provides a constant supply of nutrient-rich water. First-time growers tend to water the plants in excess, fearing they will not receive enough water. Wick systems, passively, provide plants with the right and necessary amount of water. Passive systems are quiet and do not require electricity. Even if complete kits are available, you can assemble a wick system using materials that are available at home. And, thanks to the absence of moving parts, the danger of falling or breaking objects is really minimal.

We have already commented on the concept and advantages of a wick system. Now, let's see how you can ride yours. A small observation before going into details: the most important aspect to consider is the quality of the wick. After all, it is an essential element of the wick system. The wick material will directly affect the speed and amount of liquid that is capable of absorbing and transporting the plants.

To make the wick, you can use every day homemade materials, such as nylon rope, the strands of a mop, strips of old clothes, or strips of propylene. Beforehand, you can test these materials by experimenting with colored water. When an hour has passed, you should be able to see how far and how fast the water has traveled. And finally, to get the best results, use two wicks per plant. Fill a bowl or small bucket with nutrient-rich water. Ideally, the container should be opaque and have a slightly smaller circumference than the growing pot.

Then, take the pot where you are going to plant and place both wicks in the center. A small hole should be in the base of the pot where the wicks can hang. Fill the pot with the chosen culture substrate and make sure the wicks are long enough to come into contact with the plant's root system and at the same time, be submerged in the fertilizer solution.

It is important to adjust the length of the wick. When you are satisfied, place the pot with the plant on the container of step 1, so that the pot is suspended over the water, with the wicks partially submerged in it.

You just assembled your first wick system! You will have to look at the level of the liquid mixture in the tank to know when you need to replenish it. The frequency between filling and filling will vary depending on the thirst of the plants.

Advantages

- The main advantage of the hydroponic wick system is that it is simple to build and easy to maintain.

- If you choose to keep it small or expand it, you can do it by recycling common household items and materials.

- Another important advantage is that it does not require electricity. This makes it possible to establish a hydroponic wick system in places that lack access to electricity, as well as make it more sustainable by not consuming electricity for artificial lighting.

- Speaking of sustainability, the hydroponic wick system is very efficient in the use of water. The system regulates itself since the supply of the water-based solution depends on the consumption of the solution by the plants themselves.

- In addition, hydroponic wick systems use less water and nutrients than other crop systems, due to the types of plants it supports.

Disadvantages

Throughout this article, we have mentioned the advantages of this system. But, despite its simplicity, it has certain drawbacks and limitations:

- Not suitable for larger and thirsty plants.

- The culture substrate can retain nutrients, causing the toxic accumulation.

- The water in the tank can remain stagnant.

- If the tank is sealed, providing oxygen to the roots can be a problem.

- The liquid mixture must be analyzed often to ensure an adequate pH.

To avoid some of these inconveniences, a water pump connected to an air stone can be added. It will oxygenate the water and prevent the accumulation of waterborne diseases. However, this increases the initial cost and requires that the wick system to be close to a source of electricity. By including the water pump, the system ceases to be passive.

Nutrient Film Technique

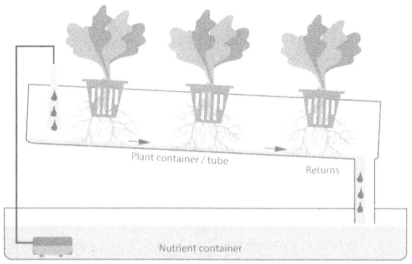

An NFT system is a hydroponic system of hydroponic culture. NFT stands for nutrient film technique. The technique describes a hydroponic system that supplies the plants with water and nutrients via a thin nutrient film. In other words, a nutrient solution runs down a tube and flows around the roots of a plant.

The flow of water and nutrients ensures an optimal supply of the plant. Part of the roots is suspended in the air, allowing them to absorb oxygen. The lower root system is washed around and can absorb water and essential nutrients.

A water pump boots the nutrient solution from a water reservoir to the highest point of the NFT system. From there, the nutrient solution flows through the tubes and finally falls back into the water reservoir.

The Ebb and Flow System of Hydroponics

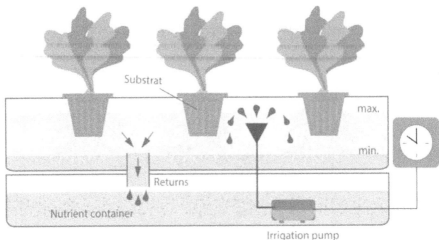

Irrigation pump

The ebb and flow system is an active and circulating system of hydroponics.

The system is active because a water pump boots the nutrient solution to the roots of the plant. In addition, it circulates because the nutrient solution flows back into the water reservoir after the flood, and the process then starts again.

Drip System

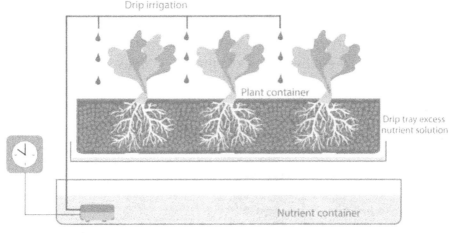

The drip system consists of a series of small pipes and droppers that connect your water tank to each of the plants in your garden. There is no limit. We could feed some plants or an industrial facility using a drip irrigation system. A timer then controls the amount of solution and the frequency of administration; neither one drop more nor one drop less is administered to the plants. You do not even have to be there to feed them.

This system still has its disadvantages. This will not be the easiest method to set up. Having a garden hose around your grow room will make things much easier for the average grower. Hoses should also be cleaned from time to time to prevent clogging. Algae and mineral buildup could stop the flow of water. This could result in one or more of your plants not getting the water solution they need. If your system distributes water under the soil, you will have no way of knowing if your plant is being nourished. You will notice a nutrient deficiency only a few days later.

Drip irrigation will also require monthly rinsing. This will help solve this problem. By regularly rinsing your system, you will clean the residue left by the slow flow of water. Finally, although this system requires less supervision, it requires more attention when you face it. You need to constantly check your plants for signs of poor health or disease. This is the only way to solve a problem in time. Particularly important for farmers living in extremely dry areas where water may be scarce. Drip irrigation will ensure you always have enough water for your plants.

Deepwater Culture

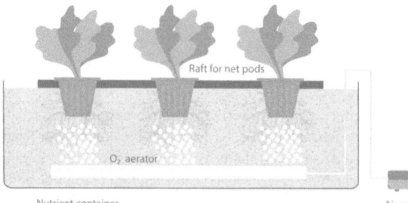

Raft for net pods

O$_2$ aerator

Nutrient container

Air pump

It is a special kind of hydroponics culture in which you grow in a ventilated nutrient solution. Here you will learn how and why more and more cannabis growers use DWC to achieve faster growth and higher yields.

While some cannabis growers simply grow their crops in the soil, other hemps use more elaborate cultivation techniques such as hydroponics. Deepwater Culture (DWC) is a hydroponic method of growing cannabis, which can have many benefits. Find out what makes a deepwater culture so rewarding and how you can set up your own DWC system!

Deepwater culture is a type of hydroponic culture that uses no medium. In a DWC system, the plants are hung in special pots or nets so that they stretch their roots down and immerse themselves in a basin of aerated, nutrient-rich water. Cultivating cannabis in a DWC system can bring many benefits compared to other farming methods.

The deepwater culture is an active hydroponic system in which the roots of the plant are suspended in a nutrient solution. Thus, the plant is always supplied with water and nutrients.

The plants are stuck in net pots and are fixed with a substrate. The mesh pots can be placed over the water surface in two ways: either you drill holes in the lid of the water reservoir, or you put the pigtails in a floating platform.

Aeroponic

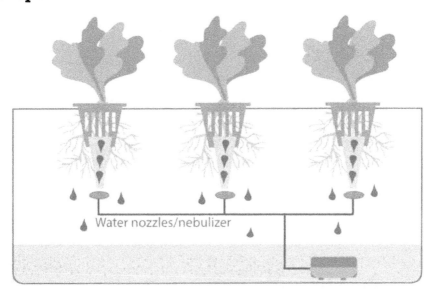

Nutrient container

Irrigation pump

This is one of the high-tech systems in hydroponic gardening. Like the NFT, the growing medium for the Aeroponic system is air. The plants' roots are misted with the nutrient solution every few minutes.

A timer triggers the misting pump, similar to the other hydroponic systems. The only difference is that there is a shorter cycle for the pump. It is a quite delicate and complicated system. There should be no interruption to misting cycles. Otherwise, the roots will dry out quickly.

CHAPTER 5.

Hydroponics vs. Aquaponics

Aquaponics

Aquaponic gardening is a food production method in which aquaculture and hydroponics are mixed. The method of raising aquatic animals such as fish, prawns, crayfish, or snails in tanks is aquaculture. The method of growing plants in a symbiotic system, in water, is hydroponics.

Over the last few decades, the supply of high-quality fish has been declining. The total number of fish available for American consumption has decreased through overfishing, habitat loss, and ecological damage. As a result, fish farms began to spring up as a way of handling the decline in the population of fish. Such fish farms have become specialists in aquaculture, rearing and cultivating aqua-life, mostly fish.

Fish farms quickly became the world's fastest-growing food industry. Aquaculture farming is very much like chicken and beef farming; there are large water systems and ponds full of water and fish. Fish farms are also used in pet stores and aquariums for bait, growing algae, and supplying fish and plants. It may also be used to increase a fish population that is endangered.

Fish farms, Mari culture, algaculture and advanced multi-trophic aquaculture are the various types of aquaculture; each of these systems produces different products and offers different uses. The culture of Mari is the cultivation of animals or plants that involve an atmosphere of saltwater. Many forms of shellfish, finfish, such as flounders, and sea plants, such as seaweed, are examples of these types of items. This type of system is developed either in the ocean, where the atmosphere is already suitable for the species, with large nets or tanks placed in the ocean water, or in tanks filled with salt water outside the ocean.

The most popular type of aquaculture is fish farms, and the purpose of this method is to produce fish for human consumption. Approximately half of the world's fish consumption comes from fish farms; in the last twenty years, this industry has tripled. Salmon, catfish, trout, cod, and tilapia are the most popular fish produced by fish farms. For the purposes of controlling the booming industry, many recent legislative acts have been produced.

Algaculture is the cultivation of algae, such as seaweed and phytoplankton. These product categories are intended for fish food, animal feed, dietary supplements, and human use. This particular type of system is very difficult to oversee, primarily the small algae, which is susceptible to small changes in the environment. Algae require a very specific lighting, temperature, and nutrition. There are two types of systems used to cultivate algae: open-pond systems and closed-pond systems. Open pong systems are primarily used because they are generally easy to construct, less expensive, and typically produce the most amount of product. However, controlling for light and temperature is difficult. Closed-pond systems are similar to open pond systems, but they are covered by controlling for both light and temperature. This type of system produces less product because it is usually smaller and more difficult to build. There are variations of different closed and open-pond systems, however, we won't cover this topic as in-depth as that.

Lastly, the integrated multitrophic aquaculture system is a more advanced system incorporating many different types of species into one system. The excrement from one species can be used as fertilizer for another species; for example, shellfish get their nutrients from shrimp and fish droppings. It is important to understand the basic components and how they work in aquaculture (or for our purposes in an aquaponic system) before starting a complex environment like this system. The purpose behind this system is balanced, you are creating a symbiotic relationship where both species benefit from each other's presence.

Hydroponics vs Aquaponics

They sound a lot alike, don't they? Hydroponics and Aquaponics? They are similar in one way, but vastly different where it counts. Hydroponics means, literally, grown in water. If you take the words aquaculture + hydroponics and put them together, you get aquaponics. Let's look at the two processes in more detail to see why one will be better for you than the other.

Ditch the soil. Both systems offer to grow a garden without soil. This represents a huge benefit. Soil becomes stagnant after years of cultivation, requiring a lot of fertilizer and/or rotation of crops. Simply replacing the soil during repetitive seasons of indoor growth becomes expensive, on top of that, the soil is easily contaminated with spores or pests laying eggs, perpetuating all of the diseases from one season to the next. Growing in the soil almost requires an outdoor garden, and living in a climate zone with harsh winters means you can only grow your veggies half of the year. Both systems offer value in growing without soil.

Instead of soil, you'll grow your plants in a biosystem of specially cultivated beneficial bacteria, and your very own circle of life will sustain both fish and plants. This healthy substitute for dirt is simple to produce, and you'll wonder why you never tried aquaponic gardening before.

Fertilize the water. Both systems require nutrient-based water for plant growth. Hydroponic gardening employs chemical nutrients, which represent constant overhead. You may obtain your growing medium from any number of suppliers, but let's face it: the uncertain role of chemicals in cancer and birth defects is generating headlines around the world. In aquaponics, you may grow organic vegetables through natural fertilizer produced by fish swimming around the tank. The advantage goes to aquaponics.

Design the right space. Both systems require light and a floor strong enough to withstand some pretty hefty weight. I was clueless. I imagined a sweet little aquarium with plants above it and was shocked to realize a twenty-gallon aquarium weighs a whopping 225 pounds. A concrete floor in the basement sounded smart, but I was hooked on the idea of cute goldfish and had a 14-ft. bay window in the dining room, so the scales became my enemy.

Figure about one inch of fish per gallon of water. If I have a fifty-gallon tank, you'll need fifty-one-inch goldfish. As they grow, that number decreases.

My research suggested that I needed at least a fifty-gallon tank, so I had to adjust my weight limits to six hundred pounds. If space and weight are an issue for you, hydroponics has the advantage in this case.

Both systems are going to affect your utility bills. The difference between them is that in hydroponics, the water may not be recycled. In aquaponics, the water must be recycled to formulate the rich growth medium to fertilize the plants. A high-water bill would make it cheaper to buy the product at the market, which makes aquaponics preferable.

Both require a growth medium that serves as an anchor for the plants, helps regulate temperature, and provides constant nourishment. In aquaponics, hydroton is a popular form made from clay. I wanted to get a product I was accustomed to using, but all of them were on the no-no list: sand, vermiculite, peat moss, wood chips, and pearlite. On the plus side, this represented a one-time purchase, and I could live with that. I see no strong value of one system over the other, because both require a mix to hold the plant.

Both systems require an investment in setting up the apparatus. A hydroponic garden is cheaper to start if you employ a wicking or water culture system. Both require a more complex design for some setups, and hydroponics equals the cost of aquaponics when you add a sump pump and additional piping. Aquaponics requires an investment in fish, but the cost will be less than continually buying chemical fertilizers for the water. In this case, the advantage goes to aquaponics.

However, the learning curve is definitely higher for aquaponic gardening. Because you are dealing with live organisms to create the fertilizer for your plants, it takes time and experimentation to get the right mix for ideal growth. If you require instant gratification, go with hydroponics. If you like a challenge, like to putter with details, and are willing to wait for results, go with aquaponics. For ease and learning the advantage goes to hydroponics.

To better asses these differences, you first have to have a clear idea of how regular gardens work.

Regular Gardening

- Plants are planted on the soil, which provides a growing medium as well as needed nutrients.

- Sunlight and rain provide other needs for photosynthesis.

- Needed nutrients and water may be supplemented by the use of fertilizers and irrigation.

Hydroponic Gardening

- Plants are placed in an inert medium.

- Water is constantly pumped through the root for hydration.

- Nutrients are introduced through specially made chemical mixes dissolved in the water.

This system is often considered more advantageous compared to regular gardening because of the level of control that can be had on the environment. There is also improved hydration and better control over the available nutrients for the plants.

The chemical mixes can be customized according to the needs of specific plants and their current stage in the growth cycle. This translates to yields that are more consistent and improve production.

Aquaponic Gardening

- It is the same with the hydroponic system with regards to the nutrition and hydration of plants. The use of chemical mixes may also be implemented to aid plant growth.

- Fish and bacteria work together to create much, if not all, of the nutrients needed by the plants.

Here, you can see that, although relying solely on fish and bacteria might not give you the exact amount of nutrients that you want, aquaponics is also much more economical.

CHAPTER 6.

Hydroponics vs Aeroponics

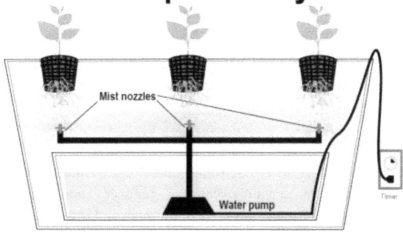

Aeroponics system

Mist nozzles

Water pump

Timer

In hydroponic cultivation, plants are grown in the absence of land and with the use of water. In general, it is possible to say that with this technique, plants grow thanks to the action of water enriched with nutrients.

In the first period, the plants are started inside inert substrates, such as coconut fiber, perlite, expanded clay, or other materials useful for the realization of substrates, to then pass into hydroponic systems, which provide, in addition to correct water supply, thanks to the presence of ad hoc lamps, the temperature, humidity and the right ventilation of the environment.

Aeroponics is an alternative form of growing plants, vegetables, and fruits that do not require the use of land or water.

With this cultivation technique, plants live and grow brilliantly and healthy thanks to a nutrient solution's nebulization, based on water and substances useful for growth, which is delivered to the roots with a special spray.

This technique should not be confused with hydroponics, where the most crucial element is not air, as in this case, but water.

Once the aeroponic system is set up, the plants are suspended with the roots in the air inside a grow room (or cultivation chamber), where they will remain until the moment of collection.

The growth and plant health basis are undoubtedly the constant control of temperature, humidity, and lighting.

Pros and Cons of Hydroponics

We have already said several times that the advantages of using a hydroponic system certainly concern reduced maintenance, the possibility of cultivating at any time of the year, and the opportunity to control the cultivation environment's climate.

More generally, the great advantage of hydroponics is in complete control over nutrients and, therefore, on plants' growth. Furthermore, hydroponically grown plants perform better than plants grown in the soil. Many systems of this type recycle water and reduce waste.

These soil-free cultivation systems use only 10% of the amount of water needed for conventional crops and are fairly easy to build and assemble. Hydroponic gardens do not require the use of herbicides or pesticides, precisely because weeds do not grow there, they need little space and do not depend on the growing seasons, because they use lamplight, which can be installed anywhere.

However, hydroponic gardens have some cons; for example, if the temperature is too high or too low, the plants could die or otherwise suffer severe damage even for a single day.

Also, the purchase of hydroponic systems and accessories may require a significant expense, especially if you are not an expert.

Pros and Cons of Aeroponics

Among the advantages of aeroponics, there is the efficiency and cleanliness of the cultivation environment in the absolute first place.

With this technique, excellent and thriving crops are obtained in a short period. Another significant advantage is the slight risk of contracting bacterial diseases and infections. On the other hand, a disadvantage, especially if you are a beginner, lies in the relatively high cost, because it requires purchasing a series of equipment. It is also necessary to have a dedicated indoor room, where you can install the aeroponic system.

Hydroponics and Aeroponics: Similarities and Differences

The hydroponic and aeroponic systems have many points in common: aeroponics is, in reality, a particular type of hydroponic culture, which also uses the benefits of air. To simplify and summarize, we can say that aeroponics is an evolution of hydroponics, to get the most out of the potential of plants in terms of yield and speed.

The main difference between the two techniques is that hydroponic systems come in many forms: plants can be suspended in water full time, or a continuous or intermittent flow can feed them. In a hydroponic system, plants grow with water and without soil, with the help of inert substrates. The two systems have in common the supply of nutrients that are delivered directly from the source and supplied to the roots.

However, the plants in aeroponics are never placed in the water but sprayed at a distance thanks to a dispenser that hydrates and nourishes the roots several times an hour, thanks to an automated system that guarantees regularity and punctuality. One reason these two cultivation methods have so much in common is that aeroponics is, in reality, a type of hydroponics. The main difference is that hydroponic systems can be of various types: there are different types, and for this, you can choose the one that best suits your needs.

A disadvantage common to both hydroponic and aeroponic cultivation systems is that relying on automated systems that require, therefore, electricity, they could require the use of expensive generators to be used in case of power outages. However, once set up and started, hydroponic and aeroponic systems allow you to save significantly compared to traditional cultivation techniques.

According to current phenomena, it is possible that forms of hydroponic and aeroponic agriculture will increase in popularity over time and become commonplace in all of our homes. What is certain is that due to climate change and man's unregulated action, the quantity of soil available for cultivation will tend to decrease, and its quality will continue to deteriorate. Therefore, more and more people will try to produce healthy food in their homes (many have already started to grow vegetables, tomatoes, strawberries, etc.). Hydroponic and aeroponic gardens and orchards can provide the right answer to these growing needs.

CHAPTER 7.

Hydroponics vs Soil Gardening

Arguments have always abounded on which is better between soil gardening and hydroponic gardening. Some people are of the opinion that soil gardening beats hydroponic gardening, while some others argue that hydroponic gardening is definitely better than soil gardening.

So, which do we believe?

Soil Gardening

Soil gardening, as you know, is more affordable because the equipment needed is just simple tools and types of machinery, nothing ambiguous. Plus, typically, you do not need to adjust so much about the soil as it does this itself, using its environment as a gage. Since plants will naturally grow in the soil, it is only natural for the soil to be gentle on plants. Overall, soil gardening seems so much easier than hydroponics, what is not to love?

Well, those are only the good sides; would you be able to deal with the bad sides?

First off, it takes longer for plants to grow in the soil. You will also notice defects late because it takes longer for these defects to become visible. What this means is that the defects would have done so much damage before they are finally noticed, ultimately making the recovery of the plants difficult and longer. This could take its toll on your money and your time.

Then, at the beginning of your plant's growth in the soil, it will require all the attention and patience as it is still tender and quite vulnerable.

You also have to deal with preventing bugs from feasting on your plants. This is an almost impossible feat, and it's better to stick with hydroponics if you can't deal with the bugs.

Hydroponic Gardening

In hydroponic gardening, you have total control over the nutrient supply provided to your plants. This will help minimize problems that usually develop from an inadequate nutrient supply in the soil.

You also skip so much growing time and get to harvest really quick because the nutrients come directly to your plants and your plants do not expend so much time and energy in search of nutrients, as is the case in soil gardening. They, therefore, spend most of the time and energy on their growth, which ends up happening fast. As a matter of fact, a plant grown hydroponically under the same conditions as one grown in the soil can grow fifty percent faster.

Plus, since your plants grow faster when grown hydroponically, you get to identify defects on time and fix them right on time.

At this point, I bet you now see just how much more beneficial hydroponics gardening is, and this is just the introduction!

Is Hydroponic Gardening Even Healthy?

The nutrients supplied in a hydroponic system are not in any way different from the one in the soil; it is gotten from mineral salts. What is different in the nutrient supply is, as I mentioned, that the roots of plants grown in the soil have to go in search of nutrients; that is what makes their root systems so large. Plants grown hydroponically do not have to do this, because the nutrients go directly to the roots and in the right amount. This lets the plant spend less time growing root systems and more time growing leaves and stems. What you get as a result is strong and healthy plants.

Gradually, more commercial growers are starting to embrace hydroponic gardening over soil gardening, because it is amazing that you can control the supply of nutrients to your plants and conserve space. This ultimately boosts yield and profit.

Plants that are grown hydroponically are also not as susceptible to diseases and pests as plants grown on the soil, because of how vigorous they are. The plants possess anti-pest and anti-fungal buffers that keep them protected. This means less money spent on fertilizers, fungicides and pesticides, and more safe foods, as the consumption of chemical-ridden plants no longer becomes an issue. Plants that have been sprayed with fungicides and other chemicals have detrimental effects on the health and this practice is worth doing away with.

Worthy of note is how much better a hydroponic system is for the preservation of the environment. Since water circulates throughout the system, it does not get sucked into the ground or evaporate quickly. So far, hydroponics has done so much for modern-day agriculture and contributed to the supply of fresh plants that are free from blemish.

This is a summary that I am sure already convinced you to consider hydroponic gardening. But just in case you are not as certain yet, we will get into the details immediately.

Why You Should Pick Hydroponic Gardening Over Soil Gardening

1. You Produce Chemical-Free Plants

When the soil is taken out of the equation, this translates to less pests and diseases to deal with. Plants grown hydroponically are not as susceptible to diseases and pests because of the absence of soil and how healthy they are. Pests tend to gravitate towards weaker plants and there are hardly weak plants in the hydroponic system, making pest infestations almost impossible. This in turn means that there is little or no need for fungicides and pesticides. In the end, you get plants that are not laden with toxic and unhealthy chemicals.

2. Saves Space

Since plants grown hydroponically rarely have bulky roots because they do not have to go in search of nutrients, you can grow more plants in smaller spaces. These plants will thrive; they have everything they need provided in the nutrient solution that is ideally measured and supplied. Planting your crops closely together rewards you with space-saving.

3. Saves Water

So much water is saved in the hydroponic gardening system. In the traditional soil garden system, a large amount of water is expended in watering the plants, this is done so that a significant part of the water gets absorbed by the soil and sucked up by the roots of the plants. Unfortunately, this system isn't such a great one because water ends up getting wasted.

How?

First off, after a good amount of water is poured out into the soil, only a reasonable amount gets to the root of the plant. The rest of the water either goes further down in the soil or evaporates. Whereas, in the hydroponic garden system, a recirculating nutrient reservoir is employed. Plant roots only take up some of the water at a time, the rest of the water is preserved for later. This preserved water in the reservoir is covered to ensure no evaporation occurs and water cannot seep through the bottom.

With this system, the amount of water that has gone into watering a plant in one day could be used for several weeks in the hydroponic system. So much water-saving!

4. Location

Unlike in the soil gardening where you have to worry about location and external environment hospitability, the case is different in hydroponic gardening. As I mentioned before, everything in the hydroponic system is under your control, you are the boss. As a result, you would not have to worry a lot about the location (you can do it anywhere); first, because you do not even need so much space, and secondly, you can control the external environment of the plant. Since hydroponic systems do not require so much space and strategic locations, you can set up your hydroponic garden in urban areas that have little space without worrying. You can also grow your plants close to the market, thus, reducing transportation costs. Regarding control of the external environment of the plants, you are in charge of the nutrient supply and the light. There are artificial lights you can use when there is little or no access to sunlight for whatever reason. The seasons have no effect whatsoever on the hydroponically grown plants because you control the environment, not the seasons. This means you can grow a plant in a season when it is difficult to grow it, this brings you more profit.

5. Impressive Growth of Plants

In soil gardening, plants take so much time and energy developing root systems for searching for nutrients, water, and oxygen. As a result, they don't grow as fast because not as much time and energy are geared towards developing the leaves, stem, and most importantly the fruit.

On the other hand, plants grown hydroponically get to grow much faster because they have all of the nutrients, oxygen, and water right at their roots (I would say at their fingertips if they had fingers, but you get the point). Since they don't have to do so much searching for nutrients, oxygen, and water, they can spend all their time growing. This way, they're grown in short periods, which means you get to have more growth cycles for other plants in a given time. Plus, the plants also grow bigger. As a result, you get more yields.

For emphasis, studies confirm that hydroponically grown plants tend to grow up to fifty percent faster and bigger than soil grown plants.

6. **Control**

Even though this has been said a lot in passing while explaining other points, this is a point too. In the soil gardening system, it is difficult to control a number of things, like the amount of water the plants get, the amount of nutrients gotten by the plants, the nutrient composition of the soil, pests, diseases, pH, etc.

In the hydroponic system, all these factors are easily regulated so you do not have to beat your head. You call the shots over what nutrients and how much your plants get, how much water your plants get and how much is preserved, the pH of the oxygenated solution, the lighting and your plants are protected from pests and diseases.

7. **No Weeding/Digging**

This is good news for some. Unlike in the conventional gardening system with soils where you have to spend so much time on dirt, taking out weeds, building mounds and the likes, there is no such thing in hydroponics.

Since you are not dealing with soil, lots of soil issues give way, one of which is weeds. It is annoyingly time-consuming to spend years doing this. With hydroponics, this problem is solved.

8. **Cleanliness**

No soil means there would be no problems. With soil comes all the unpleasant stuff like parasites, weeds, pests, and dirt. In the hydroponic system, you will not have to deal with this mess.

You can garden without getting yourself dirty.

Hydroponics is obviously the cleaner choice!

9. **Cost**

At first, the initial cost of hydroponics can look like a huge disadvantage. However, as time goes on, the ground pretty much levels up.

What do I mean?

It is much cheaper to set up a soil garden than a hydroponic system. However, along the line, soil gardening starts to cost more. Money is spent on things like fertilizers, herbicides, pesticides, fungicides, and water.

Hydroponics, on the other hand, costs more to set up, but most of these costs get cancelled out as a result of how effective the system is regarding water, land, or space use, little or no need for fertilizers, pesticides, herbicides and fungicides, quicker harvests, more yields and ultimately, more profit.

CHAPTER 8.

Is Hydroponics Only for Indoors?

Humidity

In order to maintain conditions suitable for plant growth, it is necessary to provide a number of parameters, the first of which is humidity. In conditions of high humidity, the leaves of plants grow larger. Their maximum growth is observed at 60–80%. But it is better not to stick to the extreme numbers and set the humidity at 65–75%. Cuttings will need more moisture—up to 90%, and 60% is enough for seed germination. During the late flowering, it is best to use minimal humidity to avoid mold.

Humidity is a relative concept: there is much more water in hot air than in cold air. The used percentage humidity parameter is associated with water, which air is able to hold at a given temperature. This indicator is completely unrelated to the total water content in the air. At 10° degrees F and 100%, the relative humidity of water in the air will be half as much as at the same humidity, but at 20°C. This means that any increase in temperature in the room will lead to a decrease in humidity.

Accordingly, if the lighting turns off, and the temperature drops, the humidity increases. So, darkening the room for the dark period of the cycle, it is worth running the hood for a few minutes to remove excess moisture. Otherwise, it will settle on the leaves in the form of dew and can serve as an environment in which pathogens multiply. If the lighting is on, the humidity drops, so do not immediately start the hood to keep CO2 produced at night.

If the humidity has dropped below 40%, and the air outside is too dry to raise the humidity, ventilation is indispensable: you will need a household humidifier. The air outside is usually cooler than the one in the room; therefore, once inside, it heats up and loses moisture. So even if the air outside is initially humid, it is not suitable for increasing humidity in the greenhouse.

In cold weather, it is better to cover the ventilation so that the air in the room warms up. Plants produce a lot of moisture, so it is even possible to use a dehumidifier. Plants prefer stability, so sharp changes in humidity are best avoided. If the leaves are bent up, this may be due to a rapid loss of moisture rather than an unbalanced diet, so do not rush to add corrective substances: it may be a matter of humidity.

Ventilation

Ventilation is needed, powerful and reliable, capable of updating all the air in the room in one minute. However, if the fan is too powerful, it will be difficult to ensure constant humidity. You can use an exhaust fan that can replace the air in the room in 4–6 minutes—this is enough, and the atmosphere will be stable in the room.

It is necessary to use different types of ventilation in parallel: an exhaust fan mounted on an outlet in the wall under the ceiling, it will blow air from the room; an outlet with an air intake located on the floor, in the opposite corner to the hood of the room, while the air intake must supply air from the basement or from the north wall of the house, it will not interfere with installing a protective net from dust and insects, if this does not interfere with the passage of air; circulation fans will make the air in the room homogeneous, exclude cold or hot abnormal zones, direct them better directly to the stems, which will allow air to be removed from under the crown, making the spread of diseases and insects more difficult.

The exhaust fan is calculated simply. The volume of the room in cubic meters is multiplied by 12 (updating every five minutes—12 times per hour). The resulting figure is an indicator of the corresponding fan. But there can be various barriers to the airflow. Thus, a carbon filter significantly reduces fan performance if air from the outside enters through the pipe; each of its elbows is an additional obstacle. Too small air intake will reduce fresh air. All these factors can be considered by taking a fan with a performance 25% higher than the calculated one.

Carbon Dioxide

The plant feeds on sunlight while consuming the carbon dioxide needed for photosynthesis, during which the carbohydrate necessary for the plant is formed and oxygen is released. This reaction is a source of energy for metabolism and, ultimately, for all life on Earth, since plants are food for all life forms, including humans.

But the plant also breathes, while oxygen is absorbed, which, when combined with a carbohydrate, releases carbon dioxide and energy. The plant breathes day and night, absorbing CO_2 for photosynthesis and releasing it when breathing. As a result, more oxygen is released than carbon dioxide, although oxygen is not released at night.

Gas exchange of the plant is carried out through the pores—stomata, which are located on the underside of the leaves. In dry, hot weather, stomata close and the plant slows down metabolism. But even when they are wide open, water vapor vaporized by the plant interferes with the absorption of CO_2. In the hydroponic cultivation method, the root zone has an unlimited water supply, the stomata do not close, and a good supply of carbon dioxide supports the plants in continuous growth mode.

When the first plants appeared millions of years ago, the atmosphere was much more saturated with carbon dioxide than now. Perhaps that is why the mechanism of its absorption is imperfect, and additional doses of CO_2 to plants are useful. Increased carbon dioxide helps plants withstand elevated temperatures. Permanent ventilation will ensure the flow of this gas and remove excess moisture.

Frost-Sensitive Period

Frost can kill a crop or cause serious damage. To some point, severe frosts will even reach the walls of a greenhouse, destroying plants inside. Even plants that are generally frost-tolerant can be severely damaged if the frost occurs at the wrong time of the year. Virtually all fruit or floral buds are susceptible to frosting.

If frost is likely to occur at a time near the opening of flowering buds, fruit development may be stopped even if the rest of the plant is not affected. Frost consumes some young seedlings. Tender, lush young growth is more frost-sensitive. You need to know when frosts are likely to occur at a particular site and select crops that do not have a high risk of frost damage for that site.

Day Length

Along with temperature, it is the most important factor for the formation of flower buds and for the development of fruit. For some plants, for you to achieve a good crop, the appropriate sequence of day length must take place. For other species, there must be a minimum or maximum duration of a day before flower buds develop. For example, for flowering to occur, African violets require at least 16 hours of daylight or artificial light.

Brightness

The quality of light is just as important for some plants as the duration of the light cycle. Where light intensities are too small, many vegetables and herbs do not achieve the same quality or yield amount. Other plants require lower light intensities and prefer shaded environments. A location obscured by tall trees or surrounding tall buildings will have lower light intensities than one facing off the afternoon sun. A valley site may have lower luminous intensities than one on a hill or flat plain.

The Optimal Temperature in Hydroponics

The temperature of the air is a very important external factor for the hydroponic plant cultivating place. This factor largely controls the speed of chemical reactions, enzymatic metabolism, and the development of plants (germination, a transformation of vegetative buds into reproductive buds).

The temperature that the farmer must maintain in his fields depends above all on the geographical origin of the cultivated plant. Indeed, these have special requirements in terms of temperature throughout their development: for germination, vegetative growth, and floral induction.

It should be noted that metabolism is the set of chemical transformations that take place in cells or living organisms. These reactions can be divided into two:

- **Catabolism:** The process of degradation of molecules followed by the release of energy.

- **Anabolism:** Brings together the synthesis reactions of macromolecules that demand energy consumption.

How to measure the temperature, what are the biological, chemical, physical processes depending on the temperature, and then manage this climatic factor for optimal development of the plants?

To know the temperature in his cultivating space, the horticulturist will use a thermometer. Originally, this instrument consists of a glass tube in which expends a quantity of mercury or colored alcohol. These instruments are simple and accurate enough for horticultural use. However, mercury thermometers can easily break down and spill the toxic metal into the cultivating place. With high temperatures, mercury vaporizes in the air and can be inhaled by people in the growing space.

The digital thermometers are less harmful to the environment and more convenient for the farmer. The measurement of the temperature is carried out by means of a junction diode in which circulates a constant electric field. The temperature variation of the cultivating place varies the dynamic resistance of the dipole. The temperature is displayed directly on a screen (LCD), and most of these instruments also indicate the minimum and maximum.

Some models have an external temperature sensor (probe) that allows you to know the temperature outside and inside the shelter. This is important for heating management: the greater the difference in temperature with the outside, the more it will be necessary to heat to reach the desired temperature (set temperature).

Where to Place the Hydroponic Installation?

The best place to place a hydroponic installation is an enclosed space. A basement or a greenhouse is well suited. Also, the hydroponic system can be placed in a small room without windows or in the courtyard of a private house.

The base for the installation of the structure must be strictly even and stable so that the water and the nutrient components present in it are distributed evenly. When installing the structure outdoors, pay attention to the control of liquid evaporation and ensure reliable protection of the hydroponic installation from the wind. Installing the system on the street as a whole is an extremely inconvenient option. In addition, you will have to constantly monitor that the hydroponic installation does not cool down and bring it into the room even with slight decreases in air temperature. In the case of assembling the system in the house, you will have to make more efforts to organize additional lighting.

CHAPTER 9.

Are Chemicals Used in Hydroponics?

Chemical Buffer

In the root, the respiration produced is carbon dioxide, which chemically reacts with the irrigation water to carbon dioxide (wherein an equilibrium).

In the circulating water of hydroponics, the equilibrium lies, depending on the pH, rather on the side of the free hydrogen carbonate ions (see carbonic acid pH indication water). Hydrogen carbonate ions formed to continue to react with water.

Free carbonic acid acts as a weak acid. The carbon dioxide in the circulating water lowers the pH value. In the soil, the carbonic acid reacts with limestones to calcium bicarbonate (also called bicarbonate). For details see Karst weathering.

A chemical buffer substance causes the pH to change much less when an acid (or a base) is added than would be the case in an unbuffered system. The amount of base or acid that can be trapped by a buffer without a significant change in pH is called buffer capacity that is in the soil exchange capacity.

In this specific case, a buffer substance (carbonate or a substance that also keeps metal ions as a chelate in solution) is added to the fertilizer solution. If the water contains too many protons (because it is too acidic), the buffer substance binds a proton and the reaction equilibrium is shifted to the carbonic acid, carbonic acid is formed. This breaks down into water and carbon dioxide (CO_2) and the CO_2

releases into the air (see also the carbon dioxide bicarbonate system). All fertilizer salts of a strong acid with a weak base or a strong base with a weak acid act as buffer substances, a salt of a strong base with a weak acid is used to buffer the carbonic acid.

There is also a pH increase in the microbial oxidation of ammonium to nitrate (therefore, hydroponic fertilizers should not contain any ammonium salt-based nitrogen fertilizers), they are illustrated like this:

$$NH_4^+ + 2O_2 <=> NO_3^- + 2H^+ + H_2O$$

Too high a pH-value of the circulation water can also emerge to systems such as hydroponics oxidative stress due to iron toxicity lead with various symptoms on leaves (yellowing).

In nutrient solution culture, the elongation growth of roots is inhibited at pH values below four and at too high pH values (with differences in different plant types). Nitrogen supply with NO_3^- leads to alkalization and with NH_4^+ to acidification of the rhizosphere. (See also effects of pH on plant growth and nutrient availability depending on soil pH.)

Inorganic Fertilizer

Each aqueous hydroponic fertilizer is a complete fertilizer in which all the nutrients mentioned are added artificially. That is why different formulas and approaches have been developed since the 1950s.

"Some plants grow optimally with a certain level of ion concentration ratio."

Name of the ion	Formula	Concentration in the solution [%]
Nitrate	NO 3 -	50 to 70
Hydrogen phosphate	H 2 PO 4 -	3 to 20
Sulphate	SO 4 2-	25 to 40
Potassium	K +	30 to 40
Calcium	Ca 2+	35 to 55
Magnesium	Mg 2+	15 to 30

The dosage information for liquid inorganic hydroponic fertilizers can be found on the packaging of all products.

In the case of multi-component fertilizers, the ratio of the core nutrients nitrogen (N), phosphorus (P) and potassium (K) in% of the commercially available reference base is usually given as the "NPK value," for example (13/13/21). This means that the fertilizer is 13% N, 13% P 2 0 5, and contains 21% K 2 0, see also NPK fertilizer.

Ion Exchange Granules

Ion exchange granules are solid special fertilizers (NPK full fertilizers) for long-term nutrient supply in a hydroponic system. These provide the plant with a single fertilization over several months. They consist of synthetic resin granules, which are loaded with salts (nitrates, phosphates, and potassium salts). They also contain the necessary micro-nutrients.

When normal tap water is added, the ion exchange granulate is activated. It then naturally absorbs salts contained in the tap water and releases nutrient salts loaded in the resin in exchange. The salts dissolve over a long period of time (depending on the nutrient intake of the plant), whereby the nutrient concentration remains in balance. This ensures a mild and long-lasting release of nutrients in a plant-compatible concentration.

The synthetic resin not only acts as a carrier for the nutrient salts. It functions as a buffer to keep the pH stable. It does not dissolve, but only leaves used resin granules behind.

Organic Fertilizer

Organic fertilizers are often used as a supplement to inorganic hydroponic fertilizers because inorganic fertilizers are more expensive. Organic fertilizers are mainly made from animal meals, ashes from plants or animal bones, dung from fattening animals, and industrial plant waste.

However, the exclusive use of organic fertilizer has some disadvantages, which are:

- As it is a natural product, the chemical compositions and concentrations of the nutrients vary widely. This is because; these depend on many factors, such as the food for the animal, etc.

- Organic fertilizer can be a source of various plant diseases.

- Organic fertilizer is often difficult to process due to the different consistency and size.

- Organic fertilizers give off strong smells.

- Organic fertilizers can contain ammonium compounds to reduce the ammonia (which is emitted into the air and is therefore no longer available as fertilizer nitrogen); the ammonium must be converted to nitrate in an aerobic process using microorganisms, as in aquaponics. The conversion is usually carried out in trickle filters (see plant treatment plants). Oxidation during the irrigation phase is not desirable because the aerobic process consumes oxygen, which is then missing for root respiration.

Nitrogen supply with NH 4 + instead of NO 3 - leads to reduced root biomass. However, with barley, it has been shown that the plants have to use less (sugar) energy to absorb ammonium ions than to absorb nitrate ions.

- If solid organic fertilizer is used, prior processing is necessary (crushing, sterilizing, homogenizing, etc.).

CHAPTER 10.

Fruits: The Best Plants for Your System

Fruits often require plenty of heat and water. You will need a balanced nutrient solution, with plenty of lighting and a weight supporting system. One troubling concept of these plants is that many of the vine or become top-heavy due to the fruit. You will want supports or hanging baskets to prevent any damage to the plants. Fruits also like growing at 70 degrees Fahrenheit. For melons, you will want to start with seeds, and then put the young plants in your hydroponic system, within two weeks after they start sprouting. A fruitful and nutritious formula will work best for these fruits.

Fruit trees require a lot of oxygen and water runoff. You also want plants like pineapples to grow at a pH level of 5 to 5.5. It takes two years for a pineapple to start fruiting. You can also twist the top off a pineapple plant and let new roots grow to get a new plant.

Berries are like pineapple and other fruits. They want warm temperatures, as well as 5.5 pH. It does take a year or two for the plants to mature and start bearing fruit. Most berry plants will fruit one year, grow the next, and provide fruit again in the following year.

Strawberries

If you didn't already know, strawberries do very well in wet conditions. This means that they'd do well in a hydroponic system. Since strawberries do better in the hydroponic system than in the soil, the fruits will naturally be much larger, tastier, and fresher. These fruits are known to contain vitamin C and high levels of antioxidants, which are useful in protecting and safeguarding the body from free radicals, thus boosting the immunity of the body system. It also reduces high blood pressure and high cholesterol levels.

Strawberries are well adapted for growing hydroponic crops. These fruits are, in reality, one of the most common plants grown in commercial hydroponic production. For decades, the commercial farms have developed them in large-scale NFT schemes. Nonetheless, you will also enjoy tasty fresh strawberries by cultivating them at home and picking the fruits throughout the year to feed your entire family.

Blueberries

Blueberries will typically do better in hydroponic systems than in the soil. This is a result of their need for high acidic conditions, which is difficult to navigate through with the soil gardening system. Since the grower has control over the hydroponic system, he can set the pH and nutrient content so that it is perfect for blueberries. Blueberries are known to have one of the highest levels of vitamins and antioxidants, which are useful in the protection of the body, especially the nervous system and the brain.

In Hydroponics, you will develop blueberries well, a great fruit rich in vitamins for your meal. This plant needs longer to produce seed than strawberries, even up to the second year. Usually, they're built using an NFT process. Blueberries are challenging to grow from seeds, so transplants are suggested.

Tomatoes

Tomatoes are vining plants. As a result, they are great for indoor gardens because they do not need so much space to sprout and mature. This means you can grow as much as you want in small spaces. The hydroponic growing system makes it possible to keep an eye and control the nutrient supply to the tomato plants, so that you can keep growing tomato plants throughout the year, uninterrupted, with your set-up. Tomatoes are a plant rich in vitamin A, C, and folic acid. They contain potent antioxidants that help protect against the risk of heart disease, diabetes, and cancer.

Hydroponic hobbyists and commercial farmers have widely produced several forms of tomatoes, including regular and cherry ones. Botanically, the tomato is a plant, but most people find it as vegetables, whether they are dealers or customers. One point to keep in mind is that tomatoes need a lot of sun. And if you decide to grow indoors, be prepared to purchase any grow lights.

Cucumber

Cucumbers love water, so of course, it would flourish in a hydroponic system. Cucumbers can do well, as long as you shower them with needed care and give them a little space. They are rich in nutrients like folic acid, zinc, vitamin B, vitamin C, sodium, calcium, magnesium, and potassium. Cucumbers help regulate metabolism, lower cholesterol and slow down aging.

Cucumbers are a growing plant grown at home and in commercial greenhouses. Under the appropriate circumstance, they experience fast growth and hence offer very large yields. There are many styles and sizes of cucumbers, including thick-skinned American slicers, long thin-skinned European seedless, and smooth-skinned Lebanese cucumbers. In Hydroponics, everyone will rise well. Cucumber is a warm plant, so make sure to provide ample light and temperature to it.

Eggplant

Eggplants require conditions similar to tomatoes, except that they need higher temperatures. In low temperatures that last for a long time, they easily get hurt by the weather and do not grow well. It's also better to start planting them from a nursery and in spring (early).

Sage

Sage is usually used in seasonings for meat, cheese, and sausages. Altogether, sage takes about 14 weeks from seeding to sale. It takes about eight weeks to grow from a young sprout to a mature plug. However, it will need another month or a month and a few weeks before it becomes saleable. The plants can grow to about three feet wide and, therefore, require space.

In harvesting sage, do so before they bloom, then dry them in a dryer or in a room with a perfect ventilation on screens. Be sure during this period to protect them from direct sunlight. Next up, store them in containers that are airtight. You can then sell-off.

Peppers

Peppers can grow under somewhat similar conditions to tomatoes, but increasing nighttime temperatures and declining daytime temperatures increase the yield of fruit once plants reach their mature height. Not only do peppers bring taste and spice to your diet, but they are also small in calories and rich in vitamins and nutrients. Full of vitamins A and C and a decent source of protein, folic acid, and potassium give them valuable powers in the battle against infection and disease.

Peppers need the same rising hydroponic environment as tomatoes—warm weather and significant quantities of sun. Peppers sometimes take two to three months to mature. You may either start growing them from the nearest garden supplier's seeds or plants. Jalapeno, Habanero for spicy peppers are preferred varieties for hydroponic growing; Mazurka, Cubico, Nairobi, Fellini for soft peppers.

Chapter 11.

Vegetables: The Best Plants for Your System

Beans

Beans are easy to grow as they require little maintenance and are incredibly productive. Every kind of beans, from lima beans, pole beans, green beans, and even pinto beans. For pinto beans, you will need a trellis to support the plant. In about a week, your beans should begin to germinate and you can harvest in two months.

Spinach

Spinach is a very healthy and nutritious leafy green and grows well in hydroponic systems. It grows fast and is highly prolific. This means that you would be harvesting back-to-back if you are dedicated enough, and why wouldn't you?

The vegetable contains lots of essential nutrients, like vitamin A, vitamin C, zinc, iron, fiber, vitamin E, vitamin K, protein, magnesium, and copper. Its excellent antioxidant properties help keep the heart protected and reduces aging. Spinach also enhances proper digestion and reduces cholesterol levels.

Spring Onions

For commercial growers, this is another profitable plant to grow, as harvest can happen in just three weeks. Imagine how many harvests and how much yield you would get regularly! For spring onions, they are onions, but just young ones, harvested before they are fully mature. Plus, just one onion pot can yield dozens and dozens of onions!

Spring onions are healthy, containing vitamins A, B, C, and K. Its antioxidant properties protect cellular tissue and DNA from damage. It does this by fighting against the free radicals responsible for the damage. The nutrient content of spring onions also keeps the bones healthy and is used in the treatment of colds and flus.

Lettuce

Most growers grow lettuce because of how easy it is to cultivate; it does not need so much attention, so much space, and so much growth duration. In only a few weeks, you would've harvested them and with little effort. They contain vitamin A, vitamin C, iron, potassium, vitamin K, magnesium, calcium, and phytonutrients that boost metabolism, enhances body health, and protect the body from diseases.

Chives

Chives are best grown in a hydroponic system where the pH is controlled and set to suit its slightly acidic requirements. Chives need lots of light, at least twelve hours of light every day. It typically takes eight weeks to mature and then subsequently about a month to continue harvesting after re-growing.

Kale

Lots of people have continued to attest to how effective it is to grow Kale in a hydroponic system. It has been done for years by commercial growers. The vegetable is healthy and retains its delicious nature. Hence, it can be used for both home-cooked meals and restaurant dishes. Part of the reasons Kale will do better in a hydroponic system is its need for a slightly acidic environment, which is difficult for the soil gardener to achieve. As a result, Kale plants grown hydroponically tend to look healthier than those grown in the soil.

Peas

Peas, especially snow peas (also called Chinese peas), do not do well in high temperatures. They need to be planted in fall or spring when the weather is cooler. In high temperatures, well over 80 degrees Fahrenheit, the pods set poorly because of the plant's sensitivity to heat.

Before planting peas, you will have to decide which kind you'll be planting, as there are different types of peas; there's the Garden pea

(English), Snap Peas, and the Snow peas (Chinese). Each possesses different characteristics even though they are similar. For example, the Snap peas produce edible seeds and pods, so do the Snow peas. However, the Garden peas only produce edible seeds.

You can start to harvest the peas four weeks after it starts flowering.

Broccoli

Broccoli does well in hydroponic systems, but it will require sturdy stalking because it's a heavy plant. The plant is a part of the cabbage family and is mostly perennial. May is the ideal planting season for the vegetable, and by winter, it should be ready for harvest.

Cabbage

Cabbage, depending on the variety, often needs about two feet to grow out and spread. When starting out, start in Rockwool cubes until the plants are large enough to be transferred to hydroponic pots. You know they're ready to be transferred when they are able to stand. In the hydroponic pots, make sure that they're surrounded with the controlled medium. For a flush system, it's best to fill the tray under with water and then drain immediately, you don't want the seedlings to float out of the growing medium.

Cauliflower

The cauliflower is of the same family as the kale, cabbage, broccoli, and collards. Like broccoli, cauliflower require little maintenance; it can thrive in cooler temperatures and do not need so much attention and nutrients. Since cauliflower cannot be upright, you will have to come up with a way to prevent the body of the plant from getting soaked in the hydroponic solution. An idea is using a net over the solution, so that the roots of the cauliflower can grow through the net to get to the solution. You can also try using gravel to form a layer that roots can also go through, but the body stays above. Twice a day is sufficient to supply the plant with nutrients via drip irrigation so that the roots do not get soaked.

Watercress

Watercress is a perennial crop and a part of the mustard family. It grows best between mid-autumn and spring. Harvest the watercress before it flowers, else the leaves become inedible (except it's not being grown to be eaten). Generally, they're easy to cultivate and even easier with the hydroponic system.

Parsley

A hydroponic system is perfect for parsley. The plant has a lengthy tap root and so will require a hydroponic container that is at least twelve inches to accommodate its roots.

Potatoes

Potatoes are root crops; most of their growth will happen in their root, and they will need a hydroponic system with enough depth so that they can grow effectively. As root crops, this does not mean that all their growth is directed to the roots, the foliage and stems grow too.

Potatoes will also require enough space as it grows in the root area, otherwise, their growth may become stunted.

Swiss Chard

Swiss chards are beautiful and colorful plants that can be used for your salads. They will make your meal look even more colorful than the typical green colors.

Swiss chards do well in hydroponic systems and will gladly beautify your hydroponic garden with its lovely colors. Plus, they're good for the body, as they contain phytochemicals necessary for proper body health.

Radishes

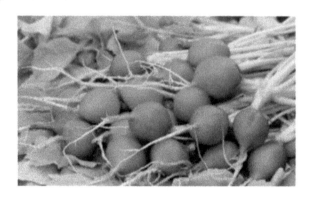

Radishes are also great with other vegetables; they add a wonderful flavor to your plate.

You will have little to no issues planting them in your hydroponic garden because they happen to be an easy-to-grow vegetable, whether it's in a hydroponic garden or a soil garden.

They typically do better in cooler temperatures and with no lights. Within a week of planting the seeds, you should begin to see its seedlings, and it's always best to start from its seeds.

Chapter 12.

Herbs: the Best Plants for Your System

It does not matter whether you cultivate herbs for therapeutic or culinary purposes; a hydroponic system is a nice way of growing them. To do so, there are several reasons: the first reason is that herbs are growing more rapidly. To this, you can also add that the herbs arise with more flavor and scent than soil-produced equivalents do. Works also reveal that hydroponic herbs produce aromatic oils more than up to 40%.

Herbs are concerned with water, temperature, and light, like the other plants. Growing herbs with hydroponics, regardless of the climate or season, help you keep producing herbs. Hydroponic processing requires less energy and eliminates the use of water.

Although all herbs in a hydroponic system should not be hard to grow, there are herbs that cultivate better. We're going to go over all of the fundamentals and advantages of each.

Basil

It is a common alternative for hydroponics, as basil is suitable to hang scent and flavor when used fresh. Those characteristics are lacking on dried basil. But having greenhouses and restaurants to use a hydroponics device for basil herbs is not unusual.

There are about 150 different basil varieties in general, although the more common ones are:

- Basil Lemon
- Sweet Basil
- Thai Sweet Basil
- Genovese Basil
- Basil Spicy
- Basil Purple
- Basil Lettuce

By propagating them or planting cuttings that shape their roots in a week, basil can be grown in both ways. It is a warm-temperature herb, so it is safest to maintain the temperature around 70–80 degrees Fahrenheit. The most used medium for developing basil with hydroponics is the Rockwool blocks. While you can use coconut coir, peat moss, vermiculite, and perlite, these can involve sterilization prior to usage.

Pythium is considered a hazard to Basil seeds. What precisely is Pythium? It destroys many herbal crops and spreads disease. Making sure your growing medium surface is not too humid is the best way to get rid of Pythium or other destroying pathogens.

When you get to harvesting the basil, the upper foliage's top 1/3 to 2/3's should be cut. The plant should keep developing that back so that you can reduce it again. Basil will grow up to 2–3 times before removing the plant entirely and starting fresh is suggested.

Only cut the quantity of basil you need; this prevents the stress of having to hold it in good shape. If you select basil, basil's shelf life is just in days, so it might be easier to keep it developing before it is needed.

Chamomile

If you're a major tea lover, you may want to learn that you can cultivate chamomile indoors on your own. Chamomile has numerous great antioxidant properties, which have been proven to reduce the likelihood of diseases such as heart failure and cancer. Often, they help combat depression and bad digestive issues.

Most would use a seed tray that can float to support the chamomile seeds to germinate. You'll want to remove the weaker ones after the seedlings expand to around 2 inches, and there's just one solid seed per cell of the tray. This may take 1 to 2 weeks for the chamomile seed to germinate. Chamomile is recommended to get light for up to 16 hours every day.

Chamomile has full versatility because it applies to pH ranges. It can vary anywhere between 5.6 and 7.5. Ideally, you'll want to reach 6.5 in the center for optimal results to rise. You should be able to yield your chamomile after about eight weeks.

The flowers may be picked by cutting off 3" of the stem and then drying them in a sunny place on a fabric. Through not picking the flowers completely, you will make replanting even easier, which helps them to seed themselves. For storage, stock your chamomile in a sealed jar in a quiet, cool place.

Rosemary

This herb with leaves that look like needles is an evergreen. The herb may flower in green, yellow, purple, or blue. Rosemary can be used as a medicine to a wide variety of problems such as:

- Heartburn

- Digestion problems

- Loss of appetite

- Headache

- Toothache

- Cough

- Low blood pressure

- High blood pressure

- Insect repellent

Compared to others, hydroponically growing rosemary can result much slower. It could take a harvest time of up to 12 weeks and the seed yields are often very small. They also result much more effective to rise hydroponically.

Such plants are susceptible to infections with the bacteria, mites, and powdery mildew. The most suitable for this plant is an NFT hydroponic system, and they can be treated at temperatures varying from 70 degrees Fahrenheit to 85 degrees Fahrenheit max.

Here are some quick tips to hydroponically cultivate the rosemary:

1. Hold the pH from 5.5–7.0.

2. Moisture levels will stay normal.

3. Provide the herb to a minimum of 11 hours of daylight.

4. You can reap 2–3 times every sowing, and that should be achieved during the year.

Oregano

Oregano is a mint, and for many years, they use this herb for medical needs and cooking. The ancient Greeks utilized Oregano for curing gastrointestinal ailments, urinary tract infections, menstrual cramps, skin problems, and dandruff. Several times they have researched Oregano for its antimicrobic action that wards off pathogenic Listeria.

Hydroponic Oregano grows well in pH levels from 6.0 to 9.0, so the level will decline between 6 and 8 for optimum performance. Rockwool cubes are commonly used to sow seeds that can take one to three weeks to germinate. The Fast Rooters, Oasis Root Blocks, or Grodan Stonewool are all other popular medium.

Oregano is a very slow grower, so it could take 8 weeks before the first harvest after transplanting. If you cultivate outside, oregano likes full heat, and as you rise below the lights, the lighting will not be different. T5 tubing are ideal for proper lighting, so they should be about two to four inches from the top of the plant to prevent the leaves from drying or burning.

Cilantro

From seedling up to the harvest of cilantro, it takes about 50 to 55 days when grown in a hydroponic system. This variety of herb needs no trimming and requires pretty much low maintenance. They can be extracted in part or as a whole.

You know what good cilantro is, too, if you're a vegetable lover. Toppings, salsas, garnishes, that's what you call it. Even if some people don't like the taste, why? The cilantro flavor is perceived differently by many people. It is characterized by some as a new and refreshing taste, whereas others consider it to be soap-like. Theoretically, here's a rundown of why this is so.

Temperatures of around 75° Fahrenheit will stay somewhere below 40° Fahrenheit. Nevertheless, with temperatures of around 60, there are higher germination speeds.

Look out for patches of bacterial leaves, accessible to cilantro. Such locations induce elevated moisture levels and susceptibility to so much humidity.

It does require lots of cooling, but it doesn't have to be overwatered. Even if it is proposed, the oscillating air recreates a sturdier natural environment.

Anise

A seldom thought of herb that has a flavor like licorice. It is also often called aniseed. Although Anise can fend off several popular problems such as digestion, nausea, and cramps, certain herbs do aid.

Although the taste of the licorice sort may make it unpopular to others, it is resourceful for bread, cakes, sausages, and cookies to be eaten. Anise seeds are very fragile and difficult to move, so it is better to encourage the seeds to germinate and expand without shifting them in their own containers. You may notice that the seeds will germinate for up to two weeks.

You want the pH level to be holding from 5.5 to 6.5. 6.0 in the center is the best place to rise. The seedlings also profit from having a wavering fan circulating the breeze softly every day for a few hours.

The easiest way to extract Anise is to cut the plant when appropriate and position it in a safe area clear of direct sunlight to dry out. This can put them upside down, too. They are harvested absolutely as early as the heads appear to look gray. Store away from the heat in an airtight jar. Anise usually has a shelf-life of 1 year.

Dill

Dill is an annual growing herb in the family of celery. In Eurasia, it is most commonly perceived as being grown where it is used to spice milk. Dried or fresh dill can be used in recipes. The stems aren't used when using dill. Growing dill is very easy hydroponically and thrives in this sort of increasing climate.

Hydroponic Growing Tips

Put the seedlings on a Rockwool and press them inward. Keep the Rockwool saturated with nutrients and water waiting for the seedlings to propagate. Propagation can take seven to ten days, but it may occur earlier.

You will then grow the Rockwool directly to your hydroponic device after germination. Maintain the pH spectrum from 5.5 to 7.5.

Enable enough space to expand and note that often dill will potentially rise as high as 3 ft.

Harvest only by cutting the green leaves and scraping the stems as ripe brown seeds emerge.

Culinary Applications for Dill

- Soups
- Sauces

- Spreads
- Casseroles
- Pickles

Medical Applications Include

- Abdominal bloat
- Relief and gas
- Cramping
- Headaches

Catnip

You could choose to raise this herb hydroponically if you have a catnip, primarily for their enjoyment and to provide yourself with some pastime. Catnip is not just used for animals, somewhat contrary to conventional myths and the word itself. Catnip has been known since the 1700s for its capacity to ease indigestion and cramps as used in teas.

The following are several suggestions for budding catnip with indoor hydroponics:

- By using leaf-tip cuttings or seeds, you can quickly propagate catnip.

- Give 5 hours of sunshine.

- Use proper irrigation to provide a constant flow of water. Catnip could be susceptible to root rot, so consider preventing an area that is too warm.

- Look out for the development of molds, which may result from so much misting.

- Eliminate all insect infestations like mealybugs, aphids, whitefly, and scale.

- Don't let the cat get close to your machine!

Benefits of Grow Herbs Hydroponically

As usual, when it comes to effectively growing plants, hydroponic systems arise as the top candidate. Herbs can mostly benefit from the capacity of the watering device to provide a continuous supply of oxygen and nutrients. In a hydroponic system, on average, herbs grow between 25 and 50% faster than an outdoor traditional soil system.

Chapter 13.

Growing Mediums, Nutrients, Temperature & Lighting

Different Types of Growing Medium for Hydroponics

Medium Originating from Rock or Stone

1. **Perlite**

Perlite is produced from volcanic rocks heated to extreme temperatures and then erupts like popcorn, resulting in a clear, porous medium. It has existed longer than any other hydroponic medium. Perlite has excellent oxygen retention, made of air-puffed glass pellets, and almost as light as air.

The main reason why it is used as a soil and soil-free mixtures substitute is its ability to retain oxygen. Perlite can be used loose forms, in pots, or in slim plastics sleeves, called "growing bags." Plants are usually installed using a drip feed system in perlite grow bags. Perlite grow bags tend to hold three or four long-term plants.

Perlite's biggest disadvantage is its lightweight consistency, making washing away easy. This disadvantage makes perlite an inappropriate medium in hydroponic systems of flood and flush type or those that would be subjected to strong winds and rains if located outside.

2. **Rockwool**

Rockwool is a molten rock derivative. It is also heated to high temperatures, but then spun into thin, insulation-like fibers. Such fibers are then compressed into cubes and slabs for hydroponic growth or sold loose as "flocks." The cubes are widely used for plant propagation, and slabs are used similarly as perlite growing bags. On the Rockwool slab, a plant is put and grown there.

The roots of the seed grow into the slab. Usually, Rockwool slabs hold three or four long-term plants. Rockwool has long been used as an alternative to fiberglass in building insulation and has been a pillar of commercial hydroponics for the past 20 years. It absorbs water readily and has solid drainage properties, which is why it is commonly used as a seed starting medium and a root cutting medium.

3. **Lightweight Expanded Clay Aggregate (LECA)**

LECA is a very coarse growing medium. Geolite, Grorox, and Hydroton are some of its common trade names. LECA consists of enlarged clay pellets, which can hold water because of their porosity and surface area.

These media are pH neutral and reusable, making them ideally suited for hydroponic systems. Although lava rocks tend to have some of the same characteristics, they should never be used in hydroponic systems because they change the pH and leave behind a thick residue that can damage different types of equipment.

4. **Vermiculite**

Vermiculite is a mineral that expands due to inter-luminary heat when exposed to high temperatures. It is rarely used alone; it is usually combined with other growth materials, especially Perlite. Vermiculite is a good medium because it allows the retention of water, moisture, and nutrients.

5. **Gravels**

Gravel is much the same as sand, with differences in particle size only. The particles of gravel are generally 2 to 15 mm in diameter, while the particles of sand are smaller but still gritty. Sand is more likely to hold water than gravel.

Organic Medium

1. Sawdust

Sawdust was commonly used in industrial hydroponics in British Columbia and Canada, primarily due to its quality. Before use, hardwood sawdust should be composted. You should never use some softwood sawdust because they contain highly toxic chemicals. For short-term growth without composting, Pinusradiata sawdust was successful.

2. Coir Fiber (Coconut Fiber)

Coir fiber has been graciously accepted as a hydroponic growing medium of high quality and is available as a thin, granular substance in several propagation cubes, blocks, Rockwool-like slabs. When used as a growing medium, coir fines should be combined with longer fibers, while fines alone are suitable for raising seeds.

Coir has a high capacity for moisture-holding and air-filled porosity and has a long-term structure. It can be used for several years as a growing medium and sterilized between crops. Some coir supplies that may be contaminated with high sodium levels should be taken good care of. To avoid this problem, hydroponic growers should always choose 'sodium-free' horticultural grade coir.

3. Composted Bark

The use of composted bark has become popular as a peat substitute, providing an excellent seed germination medium, as well as hydroponic substrates. In many cases, the bark is preferable to peat if the right grade is chosen.

Nutrient Solution for Your Hydroponic System

Without nutrients, your plants will die. It is that simple. So, your nutrient solution is the key to getting the entire system going. We touched on the simplicity of basic nutrition trumping everything else but let's go into that in more detail. Your solution can usually be broken down into two stages—growth and flower. On top of these, you can find additives to tackle different nutrient deficiencies based on the different plants you may be growing. While the budget may come into it, choosing the most expensive additives isn't a guarantee of good nutrition.

1. **Root Stimulants**

These are essential for hydroponics. Without these, you cannot get cuttings to root. These will improve the size and growth rate of your plant's roots so that they can better take up nutrients. Your plant needs the roots as structural support as well, without strong roots, it can't stand up properly or support fruit. Spindly, sickly plants are not productive because they are diverting nutrients to structure rather than leaves, blooms, or fruit. Root stimulants are also useful if your plants have root rot, as this can help grow new roots before it becomes a problem and the plant loses its means of taking up nutrition. This is an area where price often means performance and is essential for propagating cuttings and in the first stages of your plant's life.

2. **Bloom Maximizers & Vitamins**

These are additives that are high in phosphorus and potassium. These should be added on top of your base nutrient because the plant is using more of these specific elements to produce flowers. They are one of the most expensive additives and can be extremely strong. If they're not diluted properly, there's a very high chance your plant will suffer nutrient burn; however, they're also very effective at doing what they say. If you're harvesting for the flowers or you want extra flowers, start feeding as your plant shows signs of budding for best results and continue until flowering has finished.

You'll also find certain vitamins like B1 that work as a boost to the plant's immune system and prevents disease. It can also strengthen the roots against root rot and help prevent shock during the cloning process. It is essential to strong vegetative growth and helps to produce the plant's essential oils and distribution of phosphorous inside the plant cells. It helps plants at all stages of their life cycle, which is why it is an important additive.

3. Bacteria & Enzymes

As part of the plant cycle, the roots need bacteria to be able to absorb certain nutrients. These solutions contain a Mycorrhizae fungus that attaches to the roots and exchanges the plant sugars there for nutrients. Adding this to the solution helps to improve the plant absorbtion as they are the natural bacterial found in soil. You'll want a Mycorrhizae solution specifically designed for hydroponics. These are especially useful when starting a new crop or propagating because the system will be unlikely to have the necessary bacteria for good absorbtion.

You can also find enzyme solutions in the same area. Enzymes are active components in your system that break down some of the larger macronutrients into a smaller molecular form that plants can absorb better. They're also useful for preventing algae and can help plants absorb starches better, which makes for a higher sugar content in the fruit.

4. Sweetener

This is only a necessity for fruiting plants and you only need this during the flower and fruit stage. This is an extra fuel boost for your plants and can enhance the flavor. Basically, sugars fuel the microbes in the roots and improve sugar content in the plant itself. These also contain a selection of amino acids which are proteins used to build the fiber of the fruits. It is a mix of complex and simple carbohydrates at the core, but depending on the type, you may also see flavor enhancers that are specific to certain plants.

5. Flushing

Before you harvest your plant, you want to clear out the excess solutions and chemicals from it. This means you want to stop using nutrients and solutions about 4–7 days before you plan on harvesting. Flushing agents help remove the bitter chemical taste that can get left behind from heavy metals in the nutrient salts. These build up over time and will ruin the taste of your product if flushing is not done. Flushing agents help clear these out better than water alone and faster. It restores the plants' homeostasis and is essential for food crops. This should only be used in the final stage of growing right before harvesting.

Temperature

If the temperature of the plant exceeds 85 degrees Fahrenheit, the overall growth of the plants will stop quickly. If the gardener is using HID lights, then it becomes challenging to control the temperature. In order to maintain the accurate temperature, the gardener must install centrifugal fans, but in some cases, the fans alone cannot solve the problem.

For this, plan hydroponic gardening when the outside temperature is 55 degrees Fahrenheit or less. Therefore, it is possible to pull fresh air into the garden. On the other hand, you can install air conditioning.

Hydroponics Lighting System

They improve the growth of the plants; you need to have the best growing lights. This must be stated that even if fluorescent lights could give light and replace the natural lights that plants get from the sun, they cannot provide the necessary spectrum that is needed by the plants.

Their high-pressure lights, such as the sodium lights, can produce light that covers the spectrum from red to orange. They also last longer and have a lot of burning energy than the metal halide. They also use reduced energy to perform this function. However, the spectrum of light produced by this light source is quite narrow.

To get the best results, it is advised that you combine the different types of lights to get the results that are close to sunlight such as the spectrum of the sun. You can also cover an ample space with few lights using a light reflector.

Timers

Timers can be used to control lighting, the plants are affected by your lightning and so the timer is of great essence as it helps to remind you when to turn on and off your light; a timer also tells you when to turn on and off your ventilation. It also controls the nutrient flow intervals in your hydroponic garden.

Ballast

This refers to the artificial lighting that is needed in hydroponics. The ballast is a component of systems that regulates the voltage that each individual light bulb receives. Ballasts are usually electronic, digital, or magnetic.

Electronic ballasts do not use wire and steel core, rather they rely on electro components to regulate the voltage received by a bulb. On the other hand, magnetic ballasts use the electromagnetic system to regulate the amount of voltage a light bulb receives. The digital ballast is the most efficient of all, as it integrates the latest computer technology that makes it smaller and better than the others.

CHAPTER 14.

An 8-Step Formula to Raise Your Seeds Successfully

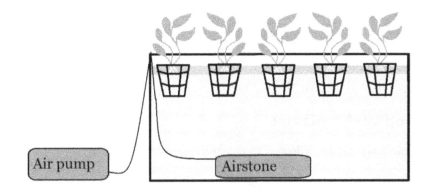

Materials

The first budget-friendly build that we are going to look at is the deep-water culture. This is one of the easiest ways that you can use to get started quickly and easily—if you can mix your nutrient solution, assemble an air pump, and put some plants into the system, you can use this sort of garden with ease! This is a great starting point for beginners because it is not technical—you are simply leaving your plants in net pots, submerged in the garden.

The system will require:

- An opaque tote storage container and lid (commonly found in 18-gallon sizes at any big-box retailer, but any size will work here if it meets the water requirements for your system)

- An air pump and air stone

- Net pots (verify that these are the right size for the full plants that you are going to be growing)

- Growing medium of choice. A common choice is using expanded clay pellets on the bottom of the net pots, with cubes of Rockwool as starters for seedlings placed atop the clay.

- Nutrient solution

- Tools to cut holes in the lid of the storage container

This build is quite simple. Remember, when assembling this, you need to have the plants ready. If you do not, then only assemble the system and wait to fill it with the nutrient solution until your plant starts.

8-Step Instructions

To build this setup, follow these steps:

1. **Gather everything that you will need:** It is always best to have everything all lined up and ready to go before starting. Make sure that the container you will be using to create your reservoir is lightproof, and if it is not, you can treat it with certain light-blocking spray paints on the exterior to try to prevent light from penetrating the nutrient solution. Also ensure that you have all of the tubing that you will need for your pump, and the right size of net pots.

2. **Prepare the growing tray:** In this system, your growing tray is more of a big tray that will suspend the growing pots into the nutrition solution. Measure out the lips of the net pots that you are going to be using and cut just slightly smaller than them. Then, cut out the holes and ensure that they fit. Make sure that your pots are assembled in the proper space as dictated by the plants that you are growing.

3. **Drill a hole for your tubing:** Near the top of the container, you are going to want to drill a small hole, just large enough for the tubing of your air pump. This will allow for the lid to sit firmly on top of the container while still providing a way for your air pump to be looped through.

4. **Add the air stone:** You want your air stone or stones at the bottom of the system. You will want each of these to work thoroughly to ensure that your water is well-mixed and aerated. Feed the tubing for the air pump through the hole you drilled and attach it to the stone with the other end attaching to the pump.

5. **Prepare the nutrient solution:** This is one of the easier steps— all you have to do is follow the instructions for the nutrient solution of your choice. You will simply read the ratios that you will be trying to mix and follow the guidelines to make it happen. Make sure that you place your container where you want it to be, as once you add the solution, it will be heavy and difficult to move. Add the nutrient solution to the container. You will want to fill it up enough so that it submerges the net pots without flooding when you add the pots at a later step.

6. **Prepare the net pots:** Now, you must prepare your net pots. This is quite simple, just fill them up with your growing medium. Then place your plants into the pots as well. The plants will be just fine if you leave them in the starting cubes of Rockwool.

7. **Put it together:** Take the lid to your system and attach it to the reservoir filled up with the nutrient solution. Place each of your net pots into the holes that you have cut. Turn on the air pump.

8. **Allow the system to run:** All that is left is to let the system run. Use lighting if necessary or leave in the sunlight if it is not. Make sure that you check water levels regularly, especially as your plants start to grow and begin to use up more water than they used to. Fill up, as necessary.

Managing Plant Nutrition

Problems fall into three possible classifications:

1. **Nutritional** – There is either too little or too much of one or more specific nutrients.

2. **Environmental** – Conditions for the environment are not ideal.

3. **Pathological** – One or more organisms tamper with the plant's health. Such organisms are called pathogenic agents.

Physiological Problems

There are several environmental factors, which, unless properly controlled, can lead to the damage of a crop. Frost or extreme supply of sunlight may burn fruit or leaves, and fruit may break, and leaves may discolor. Some of the commonest issues are detailed below.

Cracking: Lack of water or excess water may cause a split in the skin of different crops. Occasionally, newly picked carrots split up. Tomatoes that suffer from water shortage and that are exposed to high temperatures may split.

Blossom root rot: A common tomato problem is when the tomato bottom appears to be brown or black and leathery. Typically, it occurs when there is a low supply of calcium combined with erratic growth, causing stress in the plant. This problem is also associated with irregular and variable water supply and varying temperature conditions.

Crooking: This is where the fruit is warped (for example, cucumbers tend to be excessively curved). Crooking has been directly linked to poor temperature, humidity, or nutrition control.

Common Diseases and Their Control in Hydroponics

Alternaria

This blight normally affects leaves and occasionally stems. Symptoms are typically spots and often develop clustered circles as they grow. There are several varieties of Alternaria. Most of them are regulated by Zineb. A spray of copper will regulate some of these.

Anthracnose

Two different groups of anthracnose infections, which can be classified by their symptoms, are:

- Dead spots are a common symptom.

- Symptoms include abnormal growth of some parts of the plant (e.g., an elevated boundary around a depressed central area of undeveloped tissues). Different fungicides can manage anthracnose. Copper sprays control some varieties, others by Zineb and other chemicals.

Botrytis

A gray fuzzy moldy proliferation that develops on roots, branches, fruits, and berries. Botrytis occurs in damp, rainy conditions. It is necessary to remove affected parts and burn them instantly. Preventive measures include increased airflow and decreased moisture. It is possible to use thiram and dichlofluanid fungicides to control these infections.

Downy Mildew

A plant's upper leaf with this disease shows yellow discoloration or dull splotches sprouting underneath with a gray mold. It occurs under most circumstances and is regulated by Zineb.

Fusarium

Symptoms may include yellowing of the leaves, stunted growth, wilting, and dropping of leaves. Commonly, proper sanitation should regulate fusarium.

Phytophthora

There are several modes of Phytophthora ranging from the disease of new seedlings stem to other forms that affect nutrient uptake in very large plants. Symptoms are often drastic and can cause the plant to suddenly die. Remove contaminated sections and clean affected areas. Fongarid will control some modes of phytophthora effectively and reduce the spread of others.

Powdery Mildew

The disease occurs in dry, tropical, humid conditions. A chalky white growth on leaf surfaces is the principal symptom. Sulfur sprays or dust would usually provide regulation.

Water Management

Water Requirements

Plants in their habitat need both water and oxygen. Sometimes, the trick to successfully grow plants is to provide the right delicate balance between those two. Typically, too much air means too little water, and usually, too much water means insufficient air. Throughout aggregate culture, a well-drying medium (e.g., gravel) will typically be combined with a moisture-retaining medium (e.g., vermiculite) to achieve the necessary water retention balance.

Water is composed of 90 percent of the total weight in many fruits; the water content of leaves is 80 percent and that of seeds is 10 percent. In addition to its function in the plant parts, composition water is also essential for the movement of nutrients into the plant and waste products out. In a plant, everything migrates in a dissolved state. If water is not replaced constantly, the cells lose turgidity, and the plant wilts.

Excess Water

Symptoms of Excessive Water

- Development of long, slender seedlings. This usually occurs when the plants become too close together and the soil, as in glasshouses, is warm and humid.

- Presence of growth cracks (in fruits of tomatoes and heads of cabbages or carrots).

- Increased size of cells.

- Lengthy internodes (longer distances between buds and stems).

- Cells bursting (when viewed under a magnifying glass). Typically, this is due to poor irrigation or overwatering. Excess water can cause stunting, diebacks appearing on top of the plant and, in extreme cases, can lead to death. In a wet situation, there is a greater probability of infection with rots, molds, and other fungal diseases.

Symptoms of Water Deficiency

- The first and more common symptom is that the growth rate will gradually start to decline.

- Leaves gradually shrink (although no sign of discoloration).

- Later the branches get shorter, and the flowers and fruits become smaller.

- The plant also draws water from half-grown fruits of some watery fruits (e.g., strawberries, lemons, cherries, etc.) allowing the fruit to wither away.

- Appearances of diebacks from the leading shoots can happen, leading to death in extreme situations.

- A case of water shortage may be due to underwatering, poor root system, excessive drainage, or sometimes intense heat (i.e., water is sometimes dried up from the leaves faster than it can be absorbed by the roots in hot and windy conditions).

Water Relationships

Before constructing an irrigation system, an understanding of the relationship between the root environments, plants, and water is required. The root environment consists either of a solid substance consisting of particles of different sizes and shapes that mesh together imperfectly to form a dynamic system of pores and channels or an enclosed environment filled with water in either a gaseous or liquid state (or both for NFT).

With a solid material, the medium gets saturated as pore spaces are filled with water. This can happen after irrigation or rainfall. A medium will only stay saturated when there is no unrestricted draining of excess water. The amount of water that a medium can hold at saturation is dependent on the volume of available pore space. That is known as the capacity to saturate.

Moisture can be divided into three types within a stable medium:

1. **Gravity water**—This water can only last for a short time in the medium before it flows under gravitational force.

2. **Capillary water**—This is the primary source of water for plant growth, appearing on solid particles as a thin film or as particles in the pore space. The surface tension holds it up in place. (When gravity has drained all the free water, an equilibrium is achieved where the surface tension binds all the remaining water so that gravity is unable to expel it. This condition is called field capacity.)

3. **Hygroscopic water**—This is a thin film of water so firmly held to the solid particles that it cannot be absorbed by the plants. Through a process called transpiration, plants use water. The plant acts as a pump, drawing water (against the forces that hold it in the medium) into the roots of the plant, stems, and leaves from where it is lost through evaporation to the atmosphere.

Evaporation happens as water is drawn into the air and temperature, humidity and wind are determined by climatic characteristics.

If the temperatures and the rate of evaporation are high, a plant will need more water from the medium than when it is low. Plants are ready to use free water; however, there is a need for increased suction to remove surface tension holding water.

When plants reach a stage where they can no longer draw sufficient water to meet their needs, they may start dropping. This is also the wilting point. If at this stage water becomes available, the plant will recover; however, if it continues without water, it will reach a point where it is beyond recuperation.

This is regarded as the persistent point of wilting. The difference between the permanent wilting point and the moisture content of the soil is known as the water available. The amount of water retained, and the amount tightly bound, can vary from medium to medium.

When to Irrigate

The region between the wilting point and the field potential is critical in irrigation, intending to preserve the level of moisture within this zone. It has usually been observed that plants take most of their needs from the upper half of the root zone and thus only about half of the available water is expended.

Therefore, irrigation is generally required when roughly half of the water available is used up. Hence, when the medium is at field capacity, the amount of water to be applied to a crop is half the water available in the root zone of the plant. The timing of irrigation applications depends on how fast the plants use the available moisture and this is usually dependent on climatic conditions and nutrient availability.

Also important is the rate at which water is supplied through irrigation, and it is governed by medium rates of infiltration, i.e., the rate at which water passes into the medium. If it can be absorbed by the medium at a rate lower than the water is supplied, runoff may occur, and water may be wasted. The ideal situation is where the rate of application equals the rate of infiltration.

Plants greatly require water to grow and survive. Nonetheless, the amount of water needed can differ from one plant to another. The two principal factors affecting how much water a plant needs to survive are:

1. **Plant Variety**

Some certain plant types have the ability to retain water for subsequent use within their tissues. This is not possible with other plants.

2. **The setting in which the plant grows**

When there is plenty of water available around the plant, it prefers to remain moister than in open, windy, warm conditions. A plant may suffer from water shortage, but it may also suffer from an unnecessary increase in the supply of water. It is important, when watering a plant, to strike that delicate balance between too little and too much. Overwatering can be as severe as underwatering.

CHAPTER 15.

Myths about Hydroponics

Hydroponics Is a New Technology

This is a very common myth that is very popular amongst traditionalists. However, as said earlier, it is just a myth. Hydroponic gardening is a very old and ancient field. It is believed that the pharaohs of Egypt loved fruits and vegetables that were grown hydroponically. Even the famous wonder of the Ancient World, The Hanging Gardens of Babylon, were supposed to be hydroponic gardens. In India, plants are grown directly in a coconut husk, hydro at the most grassroots level. It is thus proven that hydroponic gardening is not at all a new technique but an old and ancient science of cultivation.

Hydroponics Is Artificial or Unnatural

Once again, this myth is highly popular amongst traditional thinkers. Such people think that growing plants in water is against nature and is artificial. This is absolute rubbish. The growth of plants is a real and naturally occurring thing and cannot be done artificially. Plants need certain things to grow and thrive and they normally take these things from the soil. In hydroponics, we just replace the soil with water. Plants still can absorb whatever they need from the water and grow well. Unless you consider water unnatural, then you simply cannot consider hydroponic gardening unnatural.

Hydroponic gardening does not involve any kind of genetic mutation or introduction of any unwarranted and mysterious chemicals. This is not a steroid-inducing system but a perfectly natural and safe method of growing crops.

Hydroponics Harms the Environment

This is a ridiculous myth. Hydroponic gardening does not harm the environment at all. In fact, it helps the environment. Water is one of our most precious resources and because of hydroponic gardening around 70 to 90% of water can be saved as compared to the conventional form of gardening. Hydroponic gardening also does not have any fertilizer runoff. This runoff can pollute the soil and rivers, lakes, etc.

Hydroponics Is Very Complicated and Cannot Be Done at Home Unless You Are Exceptionally Talented

Hydroponics is a very easy system of gardening that can be done by almost anyone with a love for plants. An inexpensive hydroponic system can be constructed with simple things such as a bucket, hydroponic growing medium, and hydroponic nutrients. You can definitely use advanced technology and science to create an exceptionally sophisticated hydroponic garden to produce high amounts of yield, but you can also use simple, cheap, yet effective instruments and equipment if you want to do hydroponic gardening just as a hobby. As said earlier, anyone can pick up hydroponic gardening, anyone means people of all ages.

Hydroponics is Far Too Expensive

You can definitely use expensive and advanced technology and science to create an exceptionally sophisticated hydroponic garden to produce high amounts of yield, but you can also use simple, cheap, yet effective instruments and equipment if you want to do hydroponic gardening just as a hobby. You can work on a limited budget and produce excellent and fantastic results with ease if you are dedicated to your garden.

Not Widespread and Limited to Developed Nations

This is a rather bizarre and ridiculous myth. Hydroponic gardening is done in every corner of the world.

People do hydroponic gardening in places where the climate is unsuitable for the growth of plants or in countries where the quality of soil is not suitable for a good yield. It is also commonly used in developed and developing countries, such as the USA, where the soil has been abused and is no longer cultivable. In British Columbia, 90% of all the greenhouse industry is now based upon the hydroponic gardening system.

Hydroponics Must Be Done Indoors

Hydroponics is generally cultivated indoors because people don't have a place to cultivate plants outside but rather to relax. You can easily grow a hydroponic garden outdoors as well. A benefit of constructing a hydroponic garden indoors is the fact that you can control the lights. Outdoors you need to depend on the sun for the light. It is not impossible or hard to do hydroponic gardening outdoors. It is even possible to do soil gardening inside the house if you know how to do it.

Hydroponics Don't Need Pesticides

Well, this myth is very common but unfortunately false. You do need pesticides for a hydroponic garden, but the soil-born pests are eliminated naturally because there is no soil. There are other kinds of pests that you need to protect your plants from. You should ideally only use pesticides when you feel that your plants are under attack. To avoid the attack of pests, keep a close eye on your system. Never enter the dark room when you are unclean or have come from outdoors, especially from a garden or a park.

Hydroponics Produce Huge Plants

This myth is slightly true. Every seed like every other living thing has a genetic code that has all the coding that determines the size, weight, yield, etc., of the plant that the seed will produce. Hydroponics is a well-developed system, but it is not a magical system that can force a seed of cherry tomato to grow a beefsteak tomato plant. But, it can help you to grow the best cherry tomatoes with the seed though.

It is quite hard to grow a seed to its highest point in the soil as the makeup of the soil varies from place to place. Although the components of the soil can be controlled and manipulated, you cannot have 100% control over them. However, in the case of hydroponic gardening, you have total control and freedom on the components. You can easily manipulate them, so as to grow the best plants easily. Hydroponic gardening also consumes a lesser amount of energy as compared to soil gardening. This reserved energy is used by the plants to produce more and more yield. The plants become healthy, their foliage is dense, and their flower and fruits delightful.

Hydroponics is Used Primarily for Illegal Purposes

This myth, unfortunately, has some truth in it. However, like every other thing in this world, you can use hydroponics for a good purpose, as well as a bad purpose. Sugar is a very tasty and sweet product, but if used wrongly, it can give you diabetes. Similarly, dynamite is a very useful product, but if used in an improper way, it can be dangerous. Hydroponic gardening is no different. Often, law enforcement officials talk about hydroponic gardening when talking about marijuana and such illegal substances. Many people thus form a relationship or connection between the two things and start believing that hydroponics is exclusively used to grow illegal substances. Yes, it is true that people do use hydroponic systems for illegal purposes, but people use cars for illegal purposes too. If you cannot stop using cars, you should not stop using hydroponic gardening as an alternative kind of gardening. Remember, any power is good only as long as it is in safe hands. Power itself is not corrupt. The people who use it are corrupt. Likewise, hydroponic gardening is not wrong or illegal. The corrupt people who use it for their illegal benefits are wrong.

Chapter 16.

Pest Prevention and Troubleshooting

Common Hydroponic Pests

While there are many pests that can try to make our gardens their home, there are certain pests that show up with more regularity than others. These pests fall into five key categories: spider mites, thrips, fungus gnats, whiteflies, and aphids. If you find yourself with an infestation of pests, it is a safe bet that they'll fall into one of these five categories.

Spider Mites

Out of all five types of pest, spider mites are a particularly annoying one. While they are less than a millimeter long, these little guys are actually tiny spiders. Because they are so small, they have a tendency to start damaging your plants before you even notice that they have taken up in your garden. Spider mite damage will look like tiny brown and yellow spots on the leaves of your plants. While they don't look like anything serious when there are only a couple of bites, this damage accumulates quickly to really wreak havoc on your garden.

To spot a spider mite infestation, there are two key signs to look out for. While the damage to your plants can be a telltale sign, it doesn't specifically tell you that spider mites are the problem. To spot a spider mite infestation, you should check your plants to see if you can spot any spider webbing. Another way to check for spider mites is to use a tissue or clean rag to gently wipe the bottoms of your leaves. If you come away with streaks of blood, this will tell you that you have a spider mite problem.

One way of handling spider mites is to wash your plants down with a hose or powerful spray bottle. The force of the water can often knock the mites off of your plant and drown them in the growing medium. Spider mites also have some natural enemies ranging from ladybugs to lacewings, and you may consider adding these beneficial insects to your garden to feed on the spider mite population.

Aphids

Aphids like to feed on the juices of the plant, and you can find them chewing on stems, leaves, buds, fruits, or roots. They are particularly drawn to the newest parts of the plant. If you find that your leaves are misshapen or yellowing, checking the bottom can reveal aphids. They also leave behind a sticky substance referred to as honeydew. This sweet substance can actually attract other kinds of pests, so aphids are particularly annoying little critters. This substance can also lead to the growth of fungus, like sooty mold, which can cause branches or leaves to turn an unpleasant black color. Aphids are also able to carry viruses from one plant to another, so they can help nasty pathogens to spread quicker.

Like spider mites, spraying water on the leaves can dislodge them and leave them with a hard time finding their way back to your plants. If the infestation is large, dusting your plants with flour can constipate them and help convince them it is time to move on. Wiping down your plants with a mixture of soapy water can also help to kill and drive them off.

Thrips

Like spider mites and aphids, these little guys are also tiny. Often, they are only around 5 millimeters long. It can be hard to spot these little guys, but they leave damage that is clear as day. If you start to see little metallic black specks on your leaves, you probably have some thrips snacking off your garden. Leaves that thrips attack will often turn brown and become super dry because the thrips like to suck out their juices.

Thrips are small and are either black or the color of straw. Because they are so tiny, they look like dark threads to the naked eye. They like to feed in large groups and will fly away if you disturb them. They stick their eggs into flowers and leaves and they only take a couple of days to hatch, so a thrip infestation can seem like it just happened out of nowhere.

Make sure that you inspect your plants for thrip damage and remove any that are infested. Hosing off the plants will also help to reduce their population. Ladybugs, lacewings, and minute pirate bugs all feed on thrips and can be beneficial to your garden.

Fungus Gnats

Fungus gnats are an odd one. Adult fungus gnats have no interest in harming your garden. But their larvae enjoy chewing on the roots of your plants, which slows the growth and opens the plant up for infection. In extreme cases, fungus gnat larvae can actually cause the death of plants. They really like areas with a lot of moisture and high humidity.

Adults typically live for a week and in that time lay up to 300 eggs. It takes half a week for the larvae to emerge but when they do, they start a two-week diet where their main dish is the roots of your plants. When they feed on your plants, they cause them to wilt, stunt their growth, and cause a yellowing of their leaves. These nasty little things can have many generations living off the same plant.

If you suspect a fungus gnat infestation, then you should inspect your plants by carefully turning up the soil around their stems and look for larvae. If you check a plant and it suddenly lets loose a bunch of adult gnats, then you should dispose of that plant. They really like damp soils, so make sure you aren't overwatering your plants. If you have a fungus gnat problem, then letting your potting medium drain longer will help to kill off the larvae and mess up the development of fungus gnat eggs. You can also spray your plants with a combination of peppermint, cinnamon, and sesame oils. This mixture is called flying insect killer and will help to get rid of gnats.

Whiteflies

About the same size as spider mites, whiteflies look like small white moths that take up residence on your plants. They are easier to spot, but because they fly away when you bother them, they can be hard to kill. Like aphids, they enjoy sucking the juices out of your plant and you see their damage as white spots and yellowing of the leaves.

They tend to lay 200–400 eggs in clusters on the underside of the higher leaves. These eggs hatch in about a week and unattractive little nymphs come out that crawl around on your leaves before they grow wings. These crawlers will spread out from the egg and find a place to start chewing on your leaves. They'll stay in that spot for the next week or so before growing into young adults, which will repeat the cycle of movement-feasting.

Ladybugs and lacewings enjoy eating whiteflies and so introducing them to your garden can help to kill off whitefly populations. Hosing off plants with a strong blast of water will help in reducing their numbers as well. There are a bunch of organic pesticides on the market that you can get to deal with whiteflies. These pesticides can also work for the other pests, but pesticides should be a last resort option, one that you are careful with so as not to lead to undue stress on your plants.

Preventing Pests

Let us turn our attention towards how we prevent these pests from getting into our gardens in the first place. Many of these techniques will help us to identify a possible infestation as it is trying to get started and so they offer us early warnings to prepare ourselves to battle pests. If we keep up our preventative measures and keep our eyes peeled for pests, then we can save our plants a lot of damage and ourselves a lot of time by cutting off the problem at the head.

When it comes to pests it is also important to understand that not every pest is the same. This doesn't just mean that whiteflies are different from fungus gnats. What this means is that fungus gnats on the West coast are going to be different than fungus gnats on the East coast. Not every solution for prevention or extermination will work. A certain pesticide may be used to kill gnats in the East, but the ones in the West might have grown an immunity to it.

One of the ways that we prevent pests is to make sure that we limit their ability to enter our garden in the first place. We can do this in a few ways. Insect screens go a long way to keeping out pests. We also want to limit the amount of traffic in and around our setups. If at all possible, our setups will benefit greatly if they can be protected by airlock entrances as these offer the most secure protection against both pests and pathogens. Airlocks can be doubled up to create a space before the garden in which to wipe down dirt and any insects or eggs that are catching a free ride on your clothing.

In order to see if pests are starting to show up in your garden, use sticky traps around your plants. Yellow and blue sticky traps are both useful, as they attract different pests, so you want to make sure to use both kinds for the best results. Place traps near any entrances to your garden, such as doors or ventilation systems. Also, make sure to place one or two near the stems of your plants to catch those pests that prefer snacking on the lower bits, such as aphids or fungus gnats. Get into the habit of checking these traps regularly as they can give you a great idea of what kind of life is calling your garden home.

While traps will help us to get a head start fighting any infections, they aren't a foolproof method when it comes to avoiding pests. Traps should be used together with personal spot checks. This means that you should be checking your plants for pests a couple of times a week. Take a clean cloth and check the bottom of your leaves. Check around the roots for any fungus gnat larvae. You can check the tops of leaves visually. Look for any signs of yellowing or bite marks as described above.

Make sure to remove any weeds that take up root in your garden as these plants are only going to sap your garden's resources and offer a breeding ground for pests. Also remove dead or fallen plant matter, of course. This includes leaves, but also any fruit, buds, or petals that have been dropped.

Finally, before you introduce any new plants to your garden, make sure to quarantine them first so that you can check them for pests. You can use a magnifying glass to get a closer look if you need to. Give the new plants a thorough inspection, making sure to check all parts of the plant and the potting soil before you transfer it over.

By creating a system and a schedule for inspecting your plants, you can prevent an infestation of pests from ruining your garden or causing you a lot of headaches. A vigilant eye will give you the upper hand in both preventing and dealing with any kind of problem you have with pests.

CHAPTER 17.

Starting a Hydroponic Business

You need to consider a few things when starting a hydroponic system:

Considering Space

Some of the hydroponic systems don't require too much space. You can grow an herb garden on a countertop. However, if you want a large system, then you will need a bigger space. For example, NFT is highly effective for long and narrow spaces. You may consider a large ebb and flow method if you have a big chunk of space. Before you begin the system, make sure that you write down the measurements that you have available and do not go over them.

Considering Resources

You need to consider the resources or supplies each of these systems will need. For example, a drip system will not need too many resources. On the other hand, something like NFT runs a pump and needs lighting, and it will need more resources. You should also consider just how many supplies are needed. Do you have a pump? Or you need to buy one? What about tubing? You need to consider everything cost-related. You should also consider your time as a resource. Do you want a system that can be left alone for long periods of time, or do you want one that is perfectly fine being kept for a while?

Considering Cost

Cost is another huge factor to consider. Just how much money do you want to spend on your hydroponic system? Some systems are simple, and you can build them for $10. However, some systems are quite expensive and demanding on resources. If you do not mind the cost, then an expensive system such as NFT is fine.

Considering Expandability

Also, consider just how much you want your system to scale. A wick system could be great for you if you are just getting started, but if you are looking for a system that will grow with you as you continue to learn and as you decided to expand, it may not be right for you. Essentially, you must consider how likely you are to continue to grow with your garden. If this is something that you are not going to expand upon, then some of the most stringent, smaller methods may be just fine. However, if you hope to turn this into something bigger as you get more practice, you will want to look at drip methods, NFTS, and even the ebb and flow.

Considering Reusability

You must also consider just how much reusability you want. How likely are you to reuse the garden after the first or second use? With some of the more expensive and time-consuming methods, you may find that it is not actually worth the money if you are going to use them once. If you are going to grow several harvests or make your hydroponic garden a staple in your home long-term, then an NFT or other more intensive and expensive methods may be just fine. However, if this is just an experiment with kids, then you may want to stick to some of the smaller, cheaper methods.

Conclusion

Hydroponics has a longstanding reputation as a very successful method of growing plants. The idea is that your plants get the nutrients they need from a water solution you add to their soil. Many people have come to rely on hydroponic systems for their green beans, tomatoes, melons, and more.

Indoor hydroponics has little effect on your growth during the season. Design your cultivation around the ease of your fresh food's requirements. We most want an item in winter when high-quality vegetables are not in our local supermarket. The main reason that the herbs are grown separately is because they are very small in shape and would not grow well under vineyards when the light is close to the ceiling as the grape differs. Lettuce also yields higher in a very different combination of nutrients from vineyards. Finally, the lettuce is grown on a very short harvest period of 30 to 40 days, while the vines continue to grow up to six months or longer.

Lettuce can be sown every few days to supply approximately three transplants a week. It brings you salad to pick every day. The number of plants to cultivate depends on your individual demand for fresh salads. Herbs, with the exception of basil, initially grow very slowly. It takes about 3–4 months to develop well. You can harvest them every day when they grow vigorously. For a full year, they will continue to grow.

Basil requires approximately 6 weeks to get well. The plants last up to 3 to 4 months if the basil is kept well tapped from the start. When the basil is 3 to 4 inches tall, pinch the tip of the wax or slice it after the second to the third node with a scissor. This first cut allows plants to branch rather than if it is cut later and keeps the plants from becoming woody. Then cut the tops of every shoot by 3 inches back to the next or lower set of small shoots, which fork between the stick and leaves. Take this way to give you a plant with many branches that will have less woody growth. That's the trick with rising basil that I find. I personally have cultivated basil for up to six months or longer by regularly cutting it (harvesting). If it fails to bloom, it gets old or nervous. Pinch all the buds really early to keep them smaller. Sow typically approximately four plants per cube to create a plant bunch or cluster. These can be transplanted into the rising bed for 6 to 6 inches.

When you most want tomatoes, peppers, and cucumbers in winter, schedule the cultivation accordingly from November to March. Tomatoes will start to harvest fruit no later than mid-August until mid-November. A cropping cycle lasts 7 months until the end of March. Tomatoes need to be planted for about 100 days. Start a second crop by sowing seed at the beginning of March and start harvesting in June.

Greenhouse peppers take approximately one month longer to mature than tomatoes. It is best to start them in July and in March again. You can use bush varieties less mature than greenhouse varieties for a month or so. European cucumbers take 2 months from seeding to the development of the first fruit. If you want to grow all these crops in the same hydroponic system together, begin the cucumbers in September to prepare the cucumbers by November. Thus, the seedlings transplanted to your hydroponic system all start in the same size and grow together. It helps to raise the lights above all plants at the right level. It also prevents the shading of younger plants by older plants. You'll have two crops a year in total. Start your seedlings in a separate system in your own sun, so that the current plant does not interfere with the transition.

You don't need a huge light, but an 8" fluorescent tube will suffice. Invest in a LED grow light and place it six inches from the plants.

A fan—The fan blows air through the plants to create humidity in the air. Make sure that the fan is small enough so that it doesn't blow too hard; otherwise, you will end up killing your plants.

Rubber band—The most important thing is to make sure that you have a rubber band to tighten up your pots on the wall or wherever you want to place them for easy access.

Hydroponic nutrient—The exact amount of nutrients that your plant needs depend on the size of your pot and how much water they are getting from the water reservoir. However, generally speaking, your plant should be consuming half of their total volume of nutrients per week!

If you think that hydroponics is not your cup of tea, then you are underestimating yourself as there is nothing in the world that is impossible. You just have to gain more and more information regards to hydroponics system so that you cannot do a single mistake while doing it.

It is true that there is no single secret or short-cut of doing hydroponic gardening, but you need to boost up your confidence and positive attitude so that it becomes successful.

Through this book, you have learned the whole system of hydroponics in a simple yet effective manner by which you can boost the productivity of the crops by caring like your own child.

The hydroponics system just needs skilled business-minded and devoted individuals who have a keen desire towards hydroponic gardening so that they will get success. It is not essential that doing this experience in agriculture is required, but they are ready to face every challenge regarding to hydroponic system whether it is pests, etc. If you are hard-working, diligent, meticulous, and organized, you will definitely succeed in the hydroponics system.

Appendix: Monitoring Equipment

pH Meter

pH is a measure of how alkaline or how acidic water is. A pH of 7 is neutral. pH levels that range from 1 to 6 are acidic, and levels from 8 to 14 are considered alkaline or basic.

Different plants have their preferences regarding pH levels. To ensure the best possible growth, you need to have a way of testing and then adjusting the pH level of your water.

For example:

- Cabbage likes pH levels of 7.5

- Tomatoes like a pH of 6–6.5

- Sweet potatoes like a pH of 5.2–6

- Peppers like a pH of 5.5–7

- Lettuce and broccoli like a pH of 6–7

A pH meter can be obtained from local hydroponics stores or online. You need to calibrate the sensor with the calibration powder that comes with the meter. A basic pH meter will cost you $10 to $20.

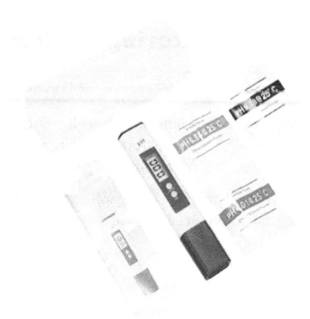

Don't use paper test strips for the water because they are inaccurate. Most of the time, a pH meter is offered in combination with a TDS or EC meter, which we will talk about next.

EC Meter

Electrical conductivity is a measurement of how easily electricity passes through the water, the higher the ion content, the better it is at conducting electricity.

All water has ions in it. When nutrients are added to the water, you are increasing the ion content, effectively increasing the electrical conductivity.

EC or Electrical Conductivity is an integral part of the hydroponics equation. The simplest way of explaining this is as a guide to salts dissolved in water. Its unit is siemens per meter, but in hydroponics, we use milli Siemens per meter.

In short, the higher the number of salts in the water, the higher the conductivity. Water that has no salt (distilled water) will have zero conductivity.

Lettuce likes an EC of 1.2 (or 1.2 milli Siemens), while basil likes an EC of 2.

That is why it is so important to know your EC and what your plants prefer, it will help you to ensure your system is at the right level.

However, electrical conductivity needs are also affected by the weather. When it is hot, the plants evaporate more water. That is why you need to decrease the EC in hot summer months. In colder winter months, you need to increase the EC.

- In warm weather, you need to decrease the EC.

- In cold weather, you need to increase the EC.

An EC meter doesn't tell you the specific amount of which mineral or fertilizer is in the water. If you only use a nutrient solution using the right ratios, you shouldn't worry.

Just because it doesn't monitor individual nutrients doesn't mean it's not useful. Salt levels that are too high will damage your plants.

You generally need to keep them between 0.8 and 1.2 for leafy greens and between 2 and 3.5 for fruiting crops like tomatoes. The source of the water can influence the EC reading. More on this later.

Sometimes, you see the recommended nutrient levels listed as CF. CF is the conductivity factor. This is like EC, used in Europe. If you multiply EC by ten, it will become CF.

For example, lettuce grows best in an EC of 0.8 to 1.2. This is a CF of 8 to 12.

TDS Meter

TDS stands for total dissolved salts. You may hear some hydroponics growers referring to the TDS and not EC. These are both used to determine the strength of your hydroponic solution. If you buy a TDS meter, there will also be an option to switch to EC readings.

It is crucial to understand that TDS is a calculated figure. TDS readings are converted from an EC reading. The problem occurs when you don't know which calculation method was used to produce the TDS; there are several different ones.

In general, EC and CF readings are used in Europe, while TDS is an American measurement. But, regardless of which measurement you choose to use, they are both effectively the same thing: a measure of the nutrient levels in your solution.

The NaCl Conversion Factor

This is effectively measuring salt in the water. The conversion factor for this mineral is your micro siemens figure multiplied by any number between 0.47 and 0.5. You'll find most TDS meters use 0.5. This is the easiest one for you to remember and calculate. Most of the meters sold will use the NaCl conversion factor.

As an example, if you have a reading of 1 EC (1 milli Siemens or 1000 micro-Siemens), you will have a TDS reading of 500 ppm.

Natural Water Conversion Factor

This conversion factor is denoted as the 4-4-2; this quantifies its contents. Forty percent sodium sulfate, forty percent sodium bicarbonate, and twenty percent sodium chloride.

Again, the conversion factor is a range, this time between 0.65 and 0.85. Most TDS meters will use 0.7.

For example, 1 EC (1000 micro-Siemens) will be 700 ppm with a TDS meter that uses natural water conversion.

Potassium Chloride, KCl Conversion Factor

This conversion factor is not a range this time. It is simply a figure of 0.55. Your EC meter reading 1EC or 1000 micro-Siemens will equate to 550 ppm.

These are not all the possible conversion options, but they are the most common. The first, NaCl is the most used today.

Dissolved Oxygen Sensor

Plant roots need oxygen to remain healthy and ensure the plant grows properly. The dissolved oxygen sensor will help you to understand how much oxygen is available in the water and ensure it's enough to keep your plants healthy.

If plants don't get enough oxygen to their roots, they can die. A minimum of 5 ppm is recommended.

A dissolved oxygen meter will be expensive for the hobbyist to buy, especially when you are starting. That is why dissolved oxygen meters are generally not purchased by people who do hydroponics for fun. A good meter can cost you $170 to $500 for a reputable brand.

You do not need to invest in one if you oxygenate the water. Oxygenation of the water can be done by using an air pump with an air stone in the water tank. Depending on the method of growing, you don't need to aerate the water.

The oxygen dissolved in the water would be at its lowest during the summer. The water heats up, and the dissolved oxygen becomes less available. While your plants can do very well in winter, they might lack oxygen during summer.

GREENHOUSE GARDENING FOR BEGINNERS

YOUR ULTIMATE AND COMPLETE GUIDE TO LEARN HOW TO CREATE A DIY CONTAINER GARDENING, GROW VEGETABLES AT HOME, AND MANAGE A MINIATURE INDOOR GREENHOUSE

Oliver Green

Introduction

Greenhouse gardening is not a modern concept. The technology and system date back to the Roman Empire. The earliest reference to the greenhouse gardening concept is directed to the Roman Emperor Tiberius. He demanded to have Armenian cucumbers every day at the royal table. Royal gardeners thought of ways to obey the emperor's order. They found out that by creating a sealed enclosure, they can control temperatures, humidity, and light exposure required by cucumbers for growth and fruit-bearing. They used a special system very similar to that of the modern greenhouses. The first modern greenhouse, with a more refined system than what the Romans used, was made in Italy in the 13th century.

During those times, having a greenhouse was limited to the wealthy. By the 19th century, greenhouses became more of an academic need. Universities put up large greenhouses, designed to hold several rare species of plants. During this time, Western civilization was starting to explore the other side of the world. Explorers and scholars were bringing back a lot of specimens from these exotic places, most of which were pretty interesting, but cannot tolerate cold climates. In order to preserve the plants in their full, natural bloom, greenhouses were the likely solution.

Greenhouse gardening can then be defined as the science of growing plants in an erected building with materials usually transparent or translucent such that the plants are provided with controlled favorable environmental conditions. Plants that are cultivated in greenhouses receive protection against conditions like soil erosion, harsh weather, violent rain and storm, plant pathogens, etc. This system of gardening is also called glasshouse or hothouse by some growers, and the major reason for setting it up is arguably to secure a considerable quantity of water vapor and heat to maintain humidity and proper temperature in the greenhouse.

The technology of greenhouse gardening serves as a viable solution to bridge the gap between the increasing world population and the increasing demand. The gap was created as a result of the urbanization of certain countries involving the construction of roads, etc., and also industrialization, which has unavoidably rendered many arable lands non-arable. The concept of the greenhouse technique is simply growing plants within a confined space under a controlled favorable environmental condition, that is, the conditions necessary for the growth of the cultivated plants are provided within the confined space regardless of the climate or season.

The growth of plants under adverse weather conditions will eventually become stunted, this is why plants grow better in a greenhouse, although the growth of plants in the greenhouse is influenced by humidity, ventilation, light, and also the rate of plant watering. The environmental condition of the greenhouse can be classified into the physical environment—which includes water, light, temperature, etc.—and the biotic environment—which includes insects, microorganisms, etc. Humidity levels above 85% in the greenhouse should, by all means, be avoided as this tends to cause more harm than good to the plants. When the humidity level in the greenhouse is too much, the plants become weak and flaccid, in which case the humid air needs to be exhausted. The need for the presence of fresh air in the greenhouse cannot be overemphasized as it encourages photosynthesis, pollination, and pest prevention. Plants generally require about 6–12 hours of light daily, therefore, in a situation where the plants in the greenhouse are not exposed to enough natural light, artificial light should be incorporated and adequately so. Also, too much supply of water in the greenhouse is just as dangerous to the plants as the lack of water supply. But factors such as growing medium, temperature, plant size, etc. contribute greatly to the determination of the amount of watering required by the plant. After you have selected the location to set up your greenhouse, the building can be self-built by placing an order for an already made "Do-It-Yourself" greenhouse kit. Setting things up in most cases is simple but in some other cases, it can also be a bit complex. For starters, not much high-tech equipment is required to practice greenhouse gardening. The greenhouse technique can be practiced simply or expanded depending on the scale of production intended.

CHAPTER 1.

What Is a Greenhouse?

A greenhouse is an age-old structure that is designed to retain heat, absorb light, and protect plants within. It can be the source for your summer starts, or it can be an option for a winter garden for year-round produce.

These simple structures have thin, clear walls made of glass, plastic panels, or plastic sheeting supported by metal, wood, or plastic structure. The skeleton is often lightweight and durable, yet strong enough to support the intended exterior. Each is designed to allow the maximum amount of light and retain as much heat and humidity as possible.

Greenhouses have changed over time to meet specific needs—large or small. A greenhouse can be as small as a plastic bottle over a seedling or as large as a multi-acre building on a massive cash crop. They can be domes, or have steep pitches, lean-to, or stand-alone structures. But, while the design and materials may vary, the intent is always the same: grow plants in the best environment possible.

Because of the heat dynamics of a greenhouse, it is possible to extend the growing season for plants to meet the needs of a market. It may mean the success of your personal garden annuals, the potential for year-round food production, or a safe place to harbor plants until they are strong enough to survive outdoors.

Types of Greenhouses

Even Span

The Even Span is the most typical design people consider when it comes to greenhouses. The name describes the construction in that the roof-line has an Even Span from the center peak to the eaves and this pitch runs the full length of the structure. Regardless of how deep the structure is, the Even Span design allows for a continuous, simple rectangular layout inside.

The design allows for maximum direct sunlight from above. It is very efficient and provides a significant amount of space for plants inside. It is also easy to build, structurally sound, and provides enough slope to allow rainwater runoff. The American style has a single, taller peak where a similar Dutch style has two peaks along the same span. When combined eave to eave, these structures resemble a row home or townhouse and are known as a Ridge and Furrow.

Because every square foot within the base of the greenhouse can be used for plant growth, these structures are a great option for massive operations. It is easy to expand in any direction, as long as the terrain is flat and level on grade.

Lean-To

For existing structures like houses or commercial buildings, a Lean-To structure is another option. These are generally connected to the side of an exterior wall. The roof is then sloped downward away from the structure it is connected to, and a shorter wall supports the eave. The two gable end halves are enclosed with flat wall support and sealed with the same material as the rest of the structure.

These structures are best used on southern-facing walls to allow the greatest amount of sunlight in—especially during winter months. Because these are not part of the original structure, and they rely on the existing structure to provide some of the support, the Lean-To greenhouse may require some level of permitting and engineering.

One of the main benefits of the Lean-To structure is the ease of access. Because these are often built as additions to existing homes, it is possible to walk directly out of a residence and step into the greenhouse. This eliminates the need to cross vast distances to the garden as the garden may be located right outside the main structure.

Freestanding

Freestanding greenhouses are generally those that are commercially available and engineered to withstand the forces of nature without additional structural support. Some Freestanding greenhouses look similar to the Even Span design, while others resemble a geodesic dome or Quonset hut. Regardless of the shape, these are meant to host a limited number of plants and are generally large enough for one person to work comfortably inside.

The main benefit of a Freestanding greenhouse is the ability to set it up on your own without special permitting, skills, or tools. Additional perks include a limited footprint that provides the benefits of a greenhouse in areas with limited space, limited portability if it needs to be relocated, and lower cost. These structures are generally a solid choice for the average homeowner or tenant.

Because these are often assembled on-site, they may or may not have components designed for power or water. This means you may need to supply utilities with extension cords, hoses, or solar systems.

A-Frame

In areas where snow load is a major concern, the A-Frame greenhouse provides a stable environment in all types of weather. This structure is designed with a steep pitch that sheds snow to the outer edges and prevents buildup on the roof. The roof extends from the peak to the ground and can be mounded up on the edges to add support in areas with high winds.

The A-Frame uses a steeper structure to allow more sun when it is lower on the horizon during the winter months. This allows more access to heat and fewer opportunities for extreme weather failure. Some useable space is lost due to the low edges and some of the higher areas generate some wasted space. However, these are an ideal option in northern zones.

Because of the design, they can be constructed with translucent plastic sheeting and still produce the same effect as glass or plastic panels. As snow builds at the base of the triangle formed by the roof, it helps to insulate and protect the outer edges from extreme cold and high winds.

Domes and Huts

An emerging style of greenhouse is proving a natural fit for cost and space limitations. Geodesic domes are structurally sound domes made of interlocking isosceles triangle sections. These are identical to a climbing dome you might see on a playground; except they are covered in clear plastic or glass panels. They can be scaled up to just about any size without impacting the structure, and provide a significant amount of space that is not encumbered by additional structural supports or beams.

Huts also provide a form of greenhouse that can be scaled up or down depending on the need and space available. Sometimes referred to as Quonset huts, these half-cylinders create a long, tall structure that can withstand heavy snow loads and wind. The arched structural supports may be engineered trusses or basic PVC pipe, and wall coverings are often a heavy-duty clear membrane or clear plastic sheeting.

CHAPTER 2.

Benefits of a Greenhouse

Plants can be majorly cultivated using 3 different systems of cultivation; these are the in-ground system, greenhouse system, or hydroponic system of cultivation. While there is no technicality involved in the in-ground system, the greenhouse and hydroponic systems both have certain advantages over the in-ground system. Virtually any kind of plant can be cultivated in a greenhouse, but with careful selection of the plants to be grown, profit can be maximized. There are times it becomes too windy, too dark, too cold, too hot, or too rainy and it takes a miracle for plants, especially vegetables, to survive such climatic conditions. Greenhouse growers have no headache whenever the climatic condition becomes adverse because it has always been their responsibility to control the environmental condition in their greenhouse garden. The benefits are as follows:

Out of Season Production

This is perhaps the major reason many growers dabble into this system of gardening. Greenhouse gardening offers you the benefit of a longer growing season, that is, plants can be grown all year-round in a greenhouse. When "out of season" crops are made available, there is usually a huge rise in their selling prices when there is high market demand, and it consequently yields a high-profit return on the investment made. Therefore, you must carry out adequate research about the plant to be cultivated before investing in its "out of season" production. Some growers call this stage the preliminary research stage, it is to ensure that the investment you are about to make will be profitable at the end of the day. In greenhouse gardening, the plants grow faster and healthier, and therefore, can be made available early before their season, during their season, and also when they are out of season. The extended growing season is one of the major benefits derived from greenhouse gardening.

Higher Yield

When the greenhouse system of gardening is compared to the traditional open-field cultivation, the yield from a greenhouse is usually 10 times higher in quantity and quality. Although this depends on the size of a greenhouse used, also the type of plant being cultivated, and the environmental condition provided in the greenhouse if optimum. The plants in a greenhouse usually have little or no enemy such as plant diseases to fight against and so it is easy for them to grow healthily and germinate quickly. The favorable environmental condition that plants enjoy in the greenhouse is a stimulant for healthy growth and higher yield. This particular benefit from using a greenhouse is being utilized in many countries of the world where the population is constantly on the increase to ensure that there is enough food in circulation that will meet the needs of the teeming population.

Higher Quality

Another benefit that is derived from using a greenhouse system is that it gives quality yield at the end of each growing season. As stated earlier that the yield from a greenhouse is usually 10 times higher than open field cultivation in quantity and also in quality. Using a greenhouse for your plant cultivation will not only offer you the benefit of producing more yield from your cultivation, but you can also be assured that the product you will obtain will be of great quality. Higher yield and higher quality are benefits enjoyed by practicing greenhouse gardening.

Plant/Crop Reliability

Due to the absence of pests, diseases, and other plant infections in a greenhouse, the plants cultivated in the greenhouse have increased reliability. That is, there is a reduced risk of infection and the yield from the greenhouse cultivation can be trusted as clean and healthy. Also, unlike conventional gardening, the grower remains unbothered during adverse climatic conditions because the plants in the greenhouse are totally not affected by the external bad weather. The reliability of plant healthy growth is high in a greenhouse system.

Pest and Disease-Free Production

A greenhouse makes it easy to protect the plants being cultivated from pest attacks and keep them free from diseases. A good and strong greenhouse should, however, be purchased to easily achieve this and keep pests away from the plants. The protection provided by the greenhouse is another great benefit that gives the plants cultivated through this method an edge over the plants cultivated using the conventional open field.

Provides the Plants With Optimum Growing Condition

This is another benefit that plants in a greenhouse enjoy as they are provided with the optimum growing condition, and therefore, they grow faster, better, and healthier. Providing the best growing environment for your plants is a jackpot that harnesses the highest possible growth rate of the plants. Regardless of the plants being cultivated, the greenhouse provides the grower with the opportunity to supply the plants with a favorable and optimum growing environment. This growing environment can sometimes mean trapping beneficial insects inside the greenhouse because not all insects are harmful to the plants. Some are very beneficial and while these beneficial insects can come and go as they like in an open field system, an advantage of using a greenhouse is that they can be trapped inside, and therefore, continuously enhance the growth of the plants in the greenhouse.

Absence of Toxic Pesticides

In the traditional system of gardening, there is sometimes the need for the strong application of toxic pesticides to fight against certain pest attacks. These toxic pesticides, no matter how little, usually reflect on the yield at the end of the day but the good news is that there is usually no need for such application of pesticides in a greenhouse. This keeps the plants in the greenhouse fresh and also ensures clean yield at the end of the growing season. This benefit also makes it possible to produce genetically superior transplants.

Energy-Saving and Less Labor-Intensive

In a greenhouse, the application of water, light, nutrient, etc. is totally controlled by the grower. This makes it easy to control how they are supplied, unlike in conventional gardening where it is more difficult to conserve energy. The ability to conserve energy in a greenhouse helps to improve the environment at large. Greenhouse gardening also makes gardening an interesting thing to do. It makes gardening less labor-intensive and almost completely stress-free. This realization is perhaps the reason we have more home growers lately as many growers practice greenhouse gardening just for the fun of it, or better still, as a hobby.

Other benefits of using a greenhouse include the efficient utilization of nutrients, water, pesticide (if any), and also the bridging of gap in plant cultivation that exist as a result of bad climatic conditions and the presence of non-arable lands in most areas.

Chapter 3.

Planning and Constructing Your Greenhouse

Now that we have looked into how to plan the outside of your structure, we need to learn about how to plan the inside of your structure. This is the space that your plants will grow in and the space that you will see whenever you are out taking care of them. It needs to be beautiful and functional. We will look into location, size, airflow, humidity, light, heating, cooling, flooring, and glazing. We will also look into a few additional things you need to keep in mind when planning your greenhouse like safety and when to secure it from the wind.

Type, Location, and Size

First, when starting the process of planning your greenhouse, you need to make sure that you have chosen the type of greenhouse that you are going to build. This will make the rest of the decisions that you are about to make much easier.

Next, you will need to choose where your greenhouse will be located. Typically, the south side of your home is the best place to put a greenhouse. This is because it will get the best and most sunlight in this location. Be sure when choosing your location, though, that there will be nothing that blocks the sun from reaching your greenhouse. For example, if your yard is bordered by tall trees and the south side of your property never sees the sun, then your property is an exception from the fact that the south side is typically the best for greenhouses. If you do not have space on the south side, it is also okay to choose a different location. You want to ensure that you get to create a perfect greenhouse—no matter what its location is. The most important thing to consider is that the space receives a decent amount of direct sunlight throughout the day.

You also need to figure out how big you want your greenhouse to be. You will want to think about the big picture while you are making this choice. How many plants you would like to grow this year is one thing to consider, but you will also want to think about how many plants you could see yourself growing 10 years down the road. You will probably want to build your greenhouse big enough to fit your dream garden so that later on you do not have to regret making it too small. You also need to consider the space that you have available when you are making this decision. Do you have enough space in your designated location for a large greenhouse or do you need to build a structure that is on the smaller side? Do you want to take up your entire designated space with the greenhouse or would you like to leave some outdoor area to enjoy as well? When you look into answering these questions for yourself, you should be able to decide how big you would like the greenhouse that you are building to be.

The inside of your greenhouse needs to create the perfect environment for the plants that you are most wanting to grow. Because of this, when you are planning the interior of your greenhouse, you will be looking mostly into its functionality. You certainly can plan the looks of the inside of your structure, but this is nowhere near as important as how well it performs.

Airflow

Let's start looking into how to design the inside of your greenhouse practically and functionally by looking at airflow. Airflow is needed to ensure that the plants get what they need. Plants breathe in a way that is the opposite of humans. Humans breathe in oxygen and exhale out carbon dioxide. Humans need fresh air to supply oxygen where they are breathing, because breathing back in the carbon dioxide that they breathed out will do no good for sustaining life. This same principle is true with plants. Plants need carbon dioxide in the air so that they can breathe it in. When they breathe out, they release oxygen. Oxygen is not good for sustaining the life of the plants. Because of this, the air in greenhouses needs to be circulated just like it is naturally outside so that plants are breathing in the things that they actually need for them to survive.

Airflow in greenhouses is achieved mainly through the use of fans. There are quite a few options based on the types of fans and the location of fans that you will need to plant out, however. Each of these options comes with its own specific set of benefits. You will need to decide what will work best in your structure and for the plants that you are most wanting to grow.

You can arrange your fans in something called a parallel layout, which means that all of the fans are on the same side of the greenhouse and lined up parallel to each other. When they are turned on, they blow the air in the same direction which causes the air to circulate around the whole greenhouse. This method for fans is best in areas that are on flat land as it does not work well with hills.

If your greenhouse is on hilly land, you may benefit more from a fan arrangement called the series method. This is an arrangement of fans that starts at the outside of the greenhouse and moves toward the middle. It again helps to move the air in a circular motion around the greenhouse structure.

Next, let's look into the different types of fans that you can choose from:

- The first type of fan that is commonly found in greenhouses is called a basket fan. Basket fans are very powerful and have wide slots. They are strong fans, so they can circulate air well, but when they are used in sequences, they do not always provide a uniform stream of air. This can cause some plants to get a lot of airflow and others to get none at all.

- Shrouded fans are an option as well. They can provide more consistent airflow to all plants. They are also great for conserving energy, so if you are looking to "go green" with your greenhouse, shrouded fans could be a great choice.

After you choose a fan type, you will have to decide if you want your airflow to be vertical or horizontal. Both methods have their good points and not so good points:

- Vertical airflow, for example, helps to ensure that the temperature of the greenhouse stays even throughout the entire structure from top to bottom.

- Horizontal airflow is better at making sure that the humidity levels are consistent among every area of plants in the greenhouse.

Cooling and Heating

Next, let's look into cooling and heating. We know that these are two of the most important factors to look into when designing a new greenhouse. The purpose of a greenhouse is actually to extend the growing season of your plants and your garden, and one of the biggest ways that they can do this is through temperature control. When you can control the temperature of your greenhouse, you do not need to rely on the natural climate in your area for the health and success of your plants. Let's look into some things that you can do to your greenhouse so that you can control the temperature well:

- First, let's look into greenhouse heating techniques. Make sure that it is in a location that gets a lot of sunlight and that it is made from a material that allows heat to enter inside. You can also make sure that your greenhouse has no cracks that could let breezes of cold air come in.

- You could also consider using solar panels on top of your greenhouse to collect energy for heat so that you could continue along the environmentally friendly path that your greenhouse idea started.

- When you live in a cold area, you will need to plan for these things during the design process. Consider installing a heater or solar panels right away so that your plants are never hurt by painfully cold temperatures.

- The first thing to try when your greenhouse begins to get too warm is to cool it down with the fans that you use for air circulation. If this also does not work, you can buy a cover for your greenhouse to give your plants a break from the heat that the sun provides them with.

- When designing your greenhouse, you will want to make sure that you have the option to use these methods if you live in a very warm climate. You can consider walls that can be rolled up partially to allow for ventilation. You will want to make sure that your design includes fans. You may even want to consider having a cover ready for the days that you know your greenhouse will get too much sun and therefore too much heat.

Humidity

Next, let's look at the humidity in your greenhouse. If your greenhouse is too humid, you will want to make sure that you are using the horizontal fan method. This helps to circulate the air directly around the plants so that the humidity does not sit in them for too long. Another way to design your greenhouse so that humidity is never an issue is to have flooring that drains well. This will make sure that there is never excess water in your greenhouse that could lead to too much humidity in the air.

The flooring of your greenhouse is also important. As we mentioned earlier, it is important to have floor drains if you think that humidity is going to be a problem because of the climate that you live in. Besides this, though, there are many things to keep in mind when choosing a greenhouse flooring material. Let's look into the different types of materials that are commonly used in greenhouse flooring as well as what each different choice is good for.

Floors

Next, let's look into the different types of greenhouse floors as well as what each different type is good for. One popular flooring type for a greenhouse is concrete. The concrete is easy to walk on and easy to keep clean. It is also easy to slope so that you can get good drainage in your building. To have a concrete floor, you will probably have to have a concrete slab made before you build your greenhouse.

CHAPTER 4.

Miniature Indoor Greenhouses

Greenhouses come in all shapes and sizes. Some pay others to build one for them. Others buy kits and assemble the greenhouse themselves. These options can be quite expensive. The truth is most people can buy inexpensive supplies, and build their own greenhouse from scratch. You can also do so in such a way that at the end of the growing season, it can easily be taken down if you so desire.

A greenhouse can both protect from freezing temperatures, and provide sufficient heat for plant growth that would not exist if your vegetables were simply out in the open, and subject to the elements/air temperature. A greenhouse can also offer your crops protection from hail and other inclement weather. You may even be able to grow crops that typically could not survive in your area.

There are a couple of main reasons why people who like to garden may not take advantage of the benefits that a greenhouse offers. Some are turned off by the costs, and others because for weather or other reasons, they do not want a greenhouse up all year-round. In regards to cost, the models I will suggest are of minimal cost. Some who live in areas that typically receive snow, hail, and other bad weather may not want a greenhouse up year-round. If that is a concern for you, the models I will propose can rather easily be deconstructed.

I will not propose specific sizes for the frame of your greenhouse. That is up to you. Whereas some people who usually have a large area of vegetables in their back yard may want a large greenhouse, others who only want to grow 1–2 crops may choose a smaller greenhouse, possibly on their side yard, between their house and fence or another small area.

Some people may design/construct their greenhouse in such a way that it has tables or other raised platforms to grow their plants on. Such construction may be appropriate when constructing an expensive greenhouse, that one never intends to remove, and if the person has back problems and cannot get on the ground to the garden. Such design is not appropriate for an inexpensive greenhouse that you intend to deconstruct at the end of each growing season. The greenhouses that follow are intended to cover plants that are growing directly in the ground.

The first thing you need to decide is which material to use for the frame of your inexpensive greenhouse. The two best choices are white PVC pipes like you would use for an outdoor lawn watering system. The other option is untreated wooden 2 x 4's. You do not need to spend the extra money on treated lumber because the wood should not be exposed to water, and because even if water leaks onto your wooden frame, you do not want chemicals from treated lumber leaching into the ground and onto your crops. If you live in an area that typically gets strong winds in the spring, summer, or fall, wood may be a better choice for your frame. You could also combine wooden 2 x 4's and PVC for your frame where you use wood for the bottom and PVC for the sides/roof.

Let us begin by discussing a PVC frame. You can go to your local home improvement store and buy this typically in 10-foot lengths. The most convenient shape to fashion this into a greenhouse is an oval or egg-shaped greenhouse. If you want a somewhat wide and tall greenhouse, you could use two 10-piece PVC pipes, one on each side, and connecting them at the roof of the greenhouse. How many of these you will need will be determined by how long you want your greenhouse to go. I also recommend you have one piece of PVC pipe running lengthwise along the roof to fasten to the side pieces. This will increase the structural integrity of the greenhouse. You can join the connections with PVC connectors, zip ties, or even duct tape in a pinch. Then on one side of the greenhouse, fashion a door frame out of PVC pipe, as well as a door with lengths of PVC running widthwise and heightwise. The door can be fastened to the frame using zip ties.

Wooden 2 x 4's is the other practical and inexpensive option for this type of greenhouse frame. Some people use a combination of wood and PVC pipe. If this is what you want to do, I recommend you use wood for the base around the edges of your greenhouse, as well as the front where you will fashion a door, and the back. With this combination of materials, you can still make oval-shaped sides and roofs.

The other option is to make a greenhouse frame entirely out of wood. If you choose this, most people do not shape such a greenhouse-like oval, but instead, build the sides and roof like an A-frame shape with the sides directly straight up perpendicular to the ground and the two sides of the roof coming together like the shape of the letter A, much like the shape of a roof on most residential house. I should note here that sometimes people who construct their greenhouse entirely out of PVC pipe also construct it in the A-frame fashion instead of an oval shape, but the oval shape is more popular when using entirely PVC pipe for the frame.

One potential disadvantage of using wood to construct your greenhouse frame is the potential for sharp edges to damage the greenhouse plastic that we will use for the windows. Accordingly, if you use wood, try to make sure the pieces fit together well, and you may need to take a power sander to sand off any sharp edges.

If using wood, construct a door out of wood, and construct a wooden frame around the door. Attach the door to the frame with metal hinges and screws. You could install an inexpensive doorknob like you would use on an interior door of a house to keep your wooden door closed.

You need to decide how far apart to space your side supports which create the walls of your greenhouse. I recommend about every 2 ½–3 feet. If using wood, you might be tempted to space them further apart because you would think wood is stronger than PVC and therefore you do not need as many supports. I would resist this temptation because the purpose of the PVC or wood is not only to hold the frame together but to give good support to the plastic sheeting that will be used as windows.

When constructing your greenhouse frame out of wood, you could use screws or nails to fasten the pieces of wood together. When deconstructing the greenhouse, if you used screws to fasten the wood together, you should be able to relatively quickly remove the screws with a screw gun. If you intend to use nails, I recommend you use nails designed for laying form boards for concrete. These nails have two heads, one that is pounded all the way down to the base of the wood, and the other that is left exposed to make removing the nail much easier, once the concrete is set and the form boards are then removed.

Once your frame is complete, you are ready to wrap the frame in plastic greenhouse sheeting. Take care when attaching the sheeting so that you do not cut or tear it. This process will go easier/faster if you have one person on each side of the greenhouse. If you have a third person standing around doing nothing, you could even have them stand in the middle of the greenhouse. The greenhouse might be tall enough that that person in the middle might not be able to reach the sheeting with their hands. They could use a soft mop to reach up and help push the sheeting down the length of the greenhouse as the two people on both sides pull the sheeting. Start at one end of the greenhouse, pull the plastic sheeting up and over and then pull it all the way down the greenhouse.

It is then time to fasten your plastic sheeting to the bottom of the frame. It should be fastened somewhat tight, but not so tight that it cannot move a little bit which it will need to do when the temperature changes. Extend it over your greenhouse and slightly past the bottom of the greenhouse. You could use screws to fasten the sheeting to the bottom of the greenhouse frame. You could also use staples. There are also specific types of tape just for this purpose such as polypropylene batten tape. Wiring is an additional option. If using PVC for your frame, an additional way to fasten the plastic is to use one size PVC for the frame, and pieces of a larger sized PVC, cut in half, and then snap those bigger pieces over the plastic and onto the frame. For example, let us say you used half-inch PVC for the frame. Once you wrap the frame in plastic sheeting, you could then cut ¾-inch PVC in half, and take one half and snap it over the plastic and onto the ½ PVC frame.

Chapter 5.

Optimal Ecosystem in Your Greenhouse

Best Floor, Cooling, and Humidity

Airflow is very important for healthy plant growth in a greenhouse, particularly in the heat of summer as temperatures (hopefully) soar. The air needs to keep moving which will prevent heat from building up and damaging your plants.

Most greenhouses will come with vents and/or windows to help with the movement of air. A good quality greenhouse will have louver vents at ground level which draw in cold air (which is heavier than hot air) and then vents at the top which allows hot air to rise out of the greenhouse. This creates a very natural movement of air which your plants appreciate.

You are looking for a greenhouse with windows and vents that account for around ⅓ of the entire roof area. They do not all need to be at roof level and, ideally, you will want vents at different levels.

If your greenhouse is not suitably ventilated, then you are going to encourage all sorts of diseases such as fungal problems, powdery mildew, and botrytis. Worse still, a greenhouse that is too hot will end up killing some of your plants.

You can leave the door open in the summer, but this can be a security problem depending on where your greenhouse is located.

The other disadvantage of leaving a door open is that pets, particularly cats, will decide to investigate your greenhouse. Dogs, cats, and chickens will cause havoc in your greenhouse from eating plants and fruits to sitting on plants. If you do have pets and want to leave the door open, then a wire panel will keep out most animals except cats.

Window or door screens can be used to keep out unwanted visitors, but the downside of these is that they can also keep out vital pollinating insects! Cats are excellent rodent deterrents but cause their own unique brand of chaos!

Shade Cloth and Paint

This is one of the simplest ways for you to provide shade for your plants.

Shade paint is applied to the outside of your glass, and it diffuses the sun and keeps some of the heat out. Modern shade paints are very clever and will react to the sunlight. When it is raining then the shade paint remains clear, but as the sun comes out, the paint turns white, reflects the sunlight.

Shade fabric is another way to cool your greenhouse, and this is put on the outside of your greenhouse to prevent the sunlight from getting to your plants. It is best installed on the outside of your greenhouse, but you can put it inside, though it will not be as effective. When it is outside, it stops the sun's rays from penetrating your greenhouse but when on the inside the sunlight is already in the greenhouse and generating heat.

Shading alone though is not going to protect your plants from heat damage. Combine this with good ventilation and humidity control to provide your plants with the best possible growing environment.

Shade cloth is a lightweight polyethylene knitted fabric available in densities from 30–90% to keep out less or more of the sun's rays. It is not only suitable for greenhouses but is used in cold frames and other applications. It is mildew and rot resistant, water permeable, and does not become brittle over time.

It provides great ventilation and diffuses the light, keeping your greenhouse cooler. It can help reduce the need to run fans in the summer and is quick to install and remove.

A reflective shade is good because instead of absorbing the sun's rays it reflects it. This is better if you can get hold of it because it will be more efficient at keeping the greenhouse cool. The reflective shade cloth is more expensive than normal shade cloth, but it is worth the money for the additional benefits.

For most applications, you will want a shade cloth that is 50–60% density, but in hotter climates or with light-sensitive plants higher densities such as 70–80% will be necessary. A lot of people use higher-density shade cloth on the roof and lower-density cloth on the walls.

Shade cloth is typically sold by the foot or meter, depending on where you are located, though you can find it sold in pre-made sizes. These are usually hemmed and include grommets for attaching the cloth to the greenhouse.

Shade cloth with a density of 70% allows 30% of light to pass through it. For most vegetables, in the majority of climates, a shade cloth of 30–50% will be sufficient. If you are shading people, then you will want to go up to a density of 80–90%.

Airflow

Keeping the air moving in your greenhouse during summer can be difficult, particularly in larger greenhouses. Many of the larger electrical greenhouse heaters will double up as air blowers in the summer just by using the fan without the heating element is turned on.

However, using a fan is down to whether or not you have electricity in your greenhouse, which not all of us will have. Although you can use solar energy to run your fan, you will find that it is hard to generate enough energy to keep it going all day.

Automatic Vents

These are an absolute godsend for any gardener and will help keep your plants alive and stop you from having to get up early to open vents!

Automatic vents will open the windows as the temperature rises. This is usually by a cylinder of wax which expands in the heat, opening the window, and then contracts as the temperature cools which closes the window. These do have a finite lifetime, typically lasting a few years but are easily replaced.

One technique that can help keep your greenhouse cool is to damp down the paths and the floor. As the water evaporates, it will help keep the greenhouse cool.

Remember too that some plants can be moved outside in the heat of the summer which will free up space in your greenhouse and help airflow.

An alternative to wax openers is a solar-powered automatic opener. These work in a similar manner, opening the vents as the temperatures increase. These are a little bit more expensive than the mechanical auto-openers though work well.

Choosing an Exhaust Fan

For larger greenhouses, you will want an exhaust fan. This is overkill for a smaller greenhouse, but anyone choosing a larger structure will benefit from installing one.

To measure the average height, measure straight down to the floor from halfway up a roof rafter. It does not have to be precise as a few inches either way is not going to make a significant difference.

To determine the cubic feet per minute rating, you need you simply multiply the volume by 0.75. Then you will need to find a fan that is near to or greater than this value.

Be careful and double-check your calculations as a fan that is too small will not provide you with enough cooling. Together with a fan, shading cloth, or paint and damping down it will help ensure the greenhouse is kept cool and your plants thrive.

As an example, if your greenhouse is 8" x 10" with an average height of 7" this will give you a calculation of 8 x 10 x 7 which is 560 cubic feet.

So, therefore, you will need a fan that is rated at least 560 CFM for sufficient cooling.

You will also need to calculate the shutter size. Do this by dividing your fan CFM by 250 which gives a shutter size in square feet.

For greenhouses over 100 square feet or wider than 8 feet 2 shutters are required, so you will need to divide this figure by 2 to get the size for each shutter.

The fan needs to be positioned as high as possible, typically at the end opposite the door. The motor needs to be on the inside of the greenhouse, and the fan can be mounted either on the inside or outside as convenient for you.

The shutters are installed at the opposite end of the exhaust fan. For those without a motor, they are installed with the vanes opening into your greenhouse. Motorized shutters are installed with the motor on the inside of the greenhouse and the vanes open outwards.

Ventilating your greenhouse is extremely important and something many growers overlook. Plants need airflow to stay healthy. Poor airflow is a major contributing factor to fungal infections which plants such as cucumber and tomatoes are particularly susceptible to.

Ensuring your plants are not too crowded will also help a lot with airflow and preventing fungal infections.

Although your greenhouse may be too small for a fan or you may not have any electricity, at the very least you need windows though louver vents will help a lot. Making sure there is adequate ventilation in your greenhouse is vital so do not skip this step when setting up your greenhouse!

Containers or the Ground?

If you are using porous containers, you will find that you have to continue watering the crops, as the soil dries out very quickly. This can lead to wasting water and increase the cost of water. In non-porous containers, you use less water because the soil grips moisture, thus retaining enough water content for a day.

Therefore, when choosing any of those containers discussed above, they should not only satisfy the growth of crops but also provide enough drainage and porosity.

Mobility of the pots and containers is also important, especially if plan to have all-year-round crops in the garden. They should be made of lightweight material to make it easy to move them around.

Choosing the right container will contribute significantly to the growth of vegetables, herbs, and fruits in your greenhouse.

CHAPTER 6.

Heating Your Greenhouse

For most people growing will end as temperatures start to drop, even though a greenhouse can extend the growing season by a few weeks.

To grow throughout the year or to keep frost-tender plants alive over winter you will need to heat your greenhouse. Depending on what you are growing you may get away with just keeping the frost off, or you may need to heat the greenhouse to warmer temperatures. A heating mat may help you to germinate seeds, but plant growth is severely slowed in the colder months.

A greenhouse does help to keep your plants warmer, and it will help to keep frost from your plants. However, if temperatures plummet too far then no matter how well built your greenhouse, it will not keep out the frost.

Before you decide upon a heating solution for your greenhouse, you need to decide what you are growing. Different crops have different temperature requirements, and if you are growing plants that are frost hardy or tolerate cooler temperatures, then you do not need to heat your greenhouse as much.

Warmer weather crops such as tomatoes, chilies, and peppers are going to be extremely difficult to grow in a greenhouse in colder areas over winter as the heater simply will not be able to keep up. To heat your greenhouse enough, you would have to spend a fortune on heating which would simply not make the investment cost-effective.

A simple, eco-friendly way to keep your greenhouse warm is to dig out a trench down the middle of your greenhouse, cover it with palettes and then make compost in it. In smaller greenhouses, this is not going to be a huge area, but it will help to raise the temperature in your greenhouse without investing in heating equipment.

Another free heating technique is to paint some barrels, buckets, or sandbags black and leave them in your greenhouse.

The easiest way to heat your greenhouse is with an electric heater, though this does require you to have electricity in your greenhouse. Running an extension cord out is not safe so if you are installing electricity then get it done professionally and safely. It has to be waterproof if it is outside and there are likely rules and regulations in your country affecting how and where the cable can be run.

You need to ensure that your electric heat is stable and that it is away from flammable material. You also need to be cautious when watering your plants to ensure you do not damage your heater.

When using an electric heater, the air must circulate properly. This will prevent hot spots as well as cold spots and also reduce condensation. Some heaters have fans built in but others will need additional air circulation.

As the price of propane has been increasing many greenhouse owners are turning to wood or pellet stoves. These are working out to be very cost-effective even on a larger scale. You will need to check local codes and follow their requirements as well as follow common-sense safety precautions. Pellet stoves are very easy to use, often come with temperature controls, and some even have blowers that will circulate the heat.

If your greenhouse is plastic, then a wood stove is not a good idea. The stove pipe gets very hot and will melt the plastic. Ideally, your stove should be vented out through a masonry foundation or something similar rather than through glass.

Another alternative is to cover your greenhouse with plastic and line the inside with bubble wrap. This is a good solution in areas where the temperature does not drop too far in winter. However, in areas where there are months of freezing weather, this will not keep the frost out of your greenhouse.

You can buy specific insulation for your greenhouse which will help reduce heat loss and your heating bill. This is often put in place as the temperature drops and removed when spring has arrived.

There are propane, natural gas, petrol, and other heaters available and these are effective. They are getting more expensive to buy, but they do a good job in a greenhouse that cannot have electricity. Many people with smaller, garden greenhouses will use a propane heater. The advantage of these heaters is you do not need to have electricity in your greenhouse, meaning your greenhouse can be sited anywhere.

Heaters are rated in British Thermal Units or BTUs. The higher the BTU, then the more heat it gives out. You can calculate the number of BTUs you need for your greenhouse using formulas found online or heater suppliers will help you. You will need to take into account several factors including the size of your greenhouse, how hot you want the greenhouse, the heat loss of the greenhouse, and more. Getting this right means you do not waste energy heating your greenhouse or buying a heater that will not do the job.

Natural gas heaters require a gas line to be run to your greenhouse whereas propane heaters run on gas cylinders, making them the most popular heaters with home greenhouse owners.

Where to Put Your Heater?

Where you locate your heater will depend on some factors such as the location of vents and shutters, where the doors are, and more.

You need to be careful that where you site your heater is not under a water leak or anything similar.

Depending on the floor in your greenhouse it may be necessary to build a plinth to mount your heater on. This will ensure the heater is level and safe.

Consider all the factors and if you are still unsure then speak to any supplier of heaters, and they will be able to advise you.

Chapter 7.

Greenhouse Heating Tips

Obviously, you want to keep your heating costs down during winter while keeping your plants warm and alive. Here are some of my favorite tips to effectively and efficiently heat your greenhouse:

- **Bubble wrap is your friend**: Clip bubble wrap to the inside of your greenhouse frame to help reduce heat loss and block draughts. You can buy horticultural bubble wrap which is both toughened and UV stabilized. Remember that larger bubbles will let more light get into your greenhouse to your plants. This bubble wrap can also be used on tender outdoor plants and pots to protect them from frost.

- **Do not be afraid of the thermostat**: If your heater has a thermostat then use it! You can set your heater only to come on when temperatures go below a certain point. You may need to experiment with the temperature a little so that the heat kicks in and heats your greenhouse before the plants get too cold.

- **Choose the right temperature**: Most plants are not going to appreciate a tropical jungle temperature so if you are just preventing frost all you need to do is keep your greenhouse at 2°C/36°F. Some tender plants including citrus trees prefer a higher minimum temperature of 7°C/45°F as will many young plants. Delicate plants will require higher temperatures, depending on the plant.

- **Buy a thermometer**: A good thermometer that can record maximum and minimum temperatures is going to help you a lot with your greenhouse. By knowing how low the temperature drops at night you will be able to use your heater more efficiently and save yourself some money. It also helps you understand how hot your greenhouse gets during the day, so you know whether or not you need to cool it down.

- **Think about heater position**: Where you locate the heaters will influence how well your greenhouse is heated. Electric heaters are positioned away from water, and so it circulates the air around the greenhouse. With all heaters you need to be careful they do not point directly at plants and dry out the leaves.

- **Heat what you need to**: Heating a greenhouse can be expensive so if you only have a few delicate plants then put them in one place, surround them with a bubble wrap or Perspex curtain, and then heat just that area. There is no point you spending money heating a greenhouse that is mostly empty when all you need to do is heat a small area.

- **Use horticultural fleece**: On the coldest nights, a couple of layers of this will give your plants that extra bit of protection by raising their temperature a few vital degrees. Remember though to remove the fleece during the day, so the plants are well ventilated and do not overheat.

- **Ventilate**: Heating your greenhouse increases humidity, so you must have good ventilation. This will keep your greenhouse healthy and prevent the build-up of fungal diseases.

- **Water early on**: You can help reduce the humidity in your greenhouse by watering your plants earlier on in the day. Give the plants the water they need and try not to overwater or water the floor in your greenhouse unless you are damping down.

- **Use your vents wisely**: Open your greenhouse vents early in the morning on sunny days to clear condensation. Close them before the sun goes down, so you trap the warmth of the day in the greenhouse. This will help your heaters to be more efficient.

- **Use a heated propagator**: If you are germinating seeds in your greenhouse you do not need to heat the entire greenhouse unless you are starting off a lot of seeds. A heated propagation mat will help keep your seeds and seedlings warm without the expense of heating the whole greenhouse.

Depending on what you are growing and how much you want to extend your growing season you may want to heat your greenhouse. For many people though the cost is excessive and it is not practical to do so. A small paraffin or propane heater though can be enough to keep the frost out of your greenhouse, extending the growing season enough so your tomatoes, peppers, and chilies have time to ripen fully!

Types of Greenhouse Heaters

There are many different types of greenhouse heaters on the market, and we touched on these already. Let's go into more detail now on these different heaters together with their advantages and disadvantages.

Paraffin Greenhouse Heaters

Paraffin heaters are one of the most popular ways to heat a greenhouse, being both affordable and readily available. For a home gardener with a smaller greenhouse, these are ideal, but as the price of paraffin has increased in recent years, this has made these less popular.

You can buy paraffin cheaper online or in bulk, but the heaters are cheap to buy new. There is also a healthy market for used paraffin heaters, so it does make this a very affordable solution.

Paraffin heaters come in different sizes and in most models; the paraffin reservoir is large enough to last 1 day, or even 2, so they are low maintenance. Being self-contained they have no requirement for electricity, and they also give off CO_2 which your plants will appreciate.

Paraffin has become less popular in recent years because of the cost of the fuel which has become harder to obtain. However, in our Internet age, it is easier now to source this fuel, though with the concerns about climate change and emissions this type of fuel is likely to wane in popularity still further.

This type of heat is always on and is manually controlled. You can end up with the heater burning when the heat is not needed and wasting fuel. There are no temperature controls on a paraffin heater as it just burns. You can often adjust the size of the flame, but there is usually no way to turn off the heat when the greenhouse reaches a set temperature.

One disadvantage of paraffin heaters is that they give off water vapor which can encourage mold if the greenhouse is not suitably ventilated.

Electric Greenhouse Heaters

These are a great form of heating, but it does require your greenhouse to have an electricity supply. Electric heaters are controlled by a thermostat so you have greater control over the heat output, and therefore, over your running costs.

Because of the dangers of mixing water with electricity you have to make sure you get a heater that is designed to work in a greenhouse and that the electricity supply is safe and protected from water and dampness.

Electric heaters are not for everyone because of the cost of running electric cable to a greenhouse. If you are on an allotment site, then you are very unlikely to have access to electricity. Depending on local regulations you may need to hire a professional to lay the cable and use armored cable.

The advantage of an electric fan heater is that it does circulate air around the greenhouse which avoids hot and cold spots. This also helps to reduce the risk of fungal problems from poor air circulation.

Propane Gas Heaters

Run from propane bottles, these are relatively cheap to run, and propane can be refilled at many camping stores or gas stations. For a greenhouse without electricity, these are a viable solution.

You will need to ensure your greenhouse is well ventilated because propane gas heaters produce water vapor. They also produce CO_2 which your plants will appreciate.

Many propane heaters come with thermostatic controls which gives you a degree of control over your running costs.

Mains Gas Heating

This is an excellent method of heating larger greenhouses. The installation costs are high, but the running costs are reasonable.

You will need a natural gas pipe run to your greenhouse. Again, this is not for everyone, and in most cases, natural gas is not going to be a cost-effective form of heating your greenhouse.

This is most popular with commercial growers in large greenhouses and is not something most home growers will install.

CHAPTER 8.

The Essential Equipment

Location

The location of your greenhouse also depends on many factors. The first factor is the type of plant you want to grow inside your greenhouse. Tropical plants need maximum sunlight exposure so you must choose a greenhouse where sunlight comes in an appropriate amount. Most houseplants and flowers need good exposure to sunlight but not direct. Your location also depends on the climate of your area. If you live in a warm place, then you must need proper shading for your greenhouse. However, if you live in a cold area then you need maximum exposure to sunlight. Remember that the sun changes its position in different seasons. A very sunny spot in June should not get any sun exposure during the January season and you must consider this fact before choosing your greenhouse location.

Floor

You have a choice of what kind of floor or base you want for your greenhouse. Many people do not bother to cover their greenhouse base and they generally have mud or other floors where they constructed their greenhouse. This gives a natural look to your greenhouse. But it is not advisable to keep your floor open because many insects, worms, and rodents may grow inside the mud and should harm your plants. Some base constructions are available with the greenhouse construction kit and you do not need to buy extra material for your base. But if it is not available in your kit, you can buy it from the market. Concrete floors are a good option for your greenhouse's base as they make the best place to put your benches and other materials. Sometimes, wooden floors are also good for your greenhouse.

Foundation

When you are building a greenhouse, the first step is to build a foundation. This needs to be done properly for you to have a solid greenhouse that will stand the test of time.

Whatever you decide to make your foundation out of, it needs to be both level and square.

You can buy pre-made greenhouse bases, and these are worth considering, but just be aware that these still need a flat and level surface to be installed on and will still need a foundation beneath them.

When building your greenhouse base, you can either make it out of poured concrete, or you can use sand and paving stones. Both are suitable and do the job well, though the latter has the advantage of being moveable in the future if necessary.

Ensure that not only are the edges of your base square but also that the diagonal measurements between the corners are identical.

Under the base, you will need the foundation which is what supports the weight of the greenhouse, which is secured to and prevents damage in windy weather.

This is to prevent damage to your structure from the ground heaving as it freezes and melts. Your local Building Permit Agency will be able to tell you where the frost line is in your area. In warmer areas, this is only going to be a couple of inches at most, but in the colder, northern areas it can be as much as a few feet.

One good way of insulating your foundation and protecting it is to use 1" foam insulation. Put this down to your frost line to reduce heat loss through the soil, which has the benefit of reducing your heating costs.

The foundation is essential because this is what you are securing your greenhouse too. It will prevent weather damage and warping in hot or cold weather. If you do not secure your greenhouse properly, then do not expect it to last the growing season. If the greenhouse starts to warp, then you can find your panes shatter or crack and become very hard to re-fit. You can also find doors and windows become stiff and very difficult to use too.

If you have bought a new greenhouse, then any warranty will not cover damage due to not having a proper greenhouse base.

Your greenhouse is built on this foundation and base, which will ensure it is easier to erect and that it will last.

There are some different choices for the foundation, which we will discuss now.

Compacted Soil

If you compact the soil enough, then you can build your greenhouse directly on the ground, particularly if you live in an area where the ground does not freeze too badly.

A lot of greenhouses will come with an optional metal plinth that has spikes in each corner. These can be cemented into the ground to prevent the base from moving.

You will still need to level the ground though, so dig out your spirit level. It is best to use a roller or other mechanical device to compact the soil to ensure it is stable. Do not build your base out of gravel or hardcore because these are just not stable enough.

The advantage of using the soil as your foundation is that it is very cost-effective. You can also use the existing ground for growing your plants in plus drainage is a lot better.

The downside of soil is that it will allow pests into your greenhouse. You will find this particularly bad in winter as pests flock to your greenhouse for the warmth.

Perimeter Bases

This is a slightly cheaper option where you use either bricks, breeze blocks or thin paving, or edging slabs to create a foundation directly under the greenhouse frame. You can use concrete if you prefer.

The foundation is built along where the frame will run, leaving the soil in the middle of the greenhouse untouched.

While you can build the foundation directly on the soil, most people will cut out a trench and place the foundation in the trench. The advantage of this latter approach is that it is easier to level.

Slabs or Paving

This is a very popular way to build your greenhouse foundation because it keeps out the weeds and pests while giving you a good, clean growing environment.

This method involves building a base the size of your greenhouse out of paving slabs and then fixing your greenhouse to it. This type of base will last for many years and is very low maintenance.

You can screw your greenhouse to the base to provide stability in windy conditions, preventing any damage. It also provides good drainage when compared to an all-concrete base.

In the winter months, a soil floor can get damp and encourage mold to grow. A paved floor helps to keep the greenhouse both warmer and drier in the cooler months.

Providing you bed down the slabs properly with 1–2-inch of sand underneath them they are surprisingly easy to get level and will not warp or move over time.

Concrete Base

This is where you mark out where your greenhouse will be and dig down a few inches before pouring concrete in to form the base.

For larger greenhouses, this has its advantages, but it can be expensive and does require special tools such as a concrete mixer.

This is a very durable base, and you can fit expansion bolts to secure larger structures. You may have an issue with standing water so may want to consider putting drainage holes in to prevent standing water.

Frame

The frame is extremely important, because it provides the integrity of the structure, and also anchors the greenhouse covering.

The materials available for frames are:

Aluminum

This will provide a very strong frame that does not rust, and it is lightweight. It has a very long lifespan and it is the most widely used frame for greenhouses. Aluminum has extruding channels, which are perfect for inserting the covering panels.

Steel

Steel that is galvanized is very strong and long-lasting plus it is reasonably priced. Because of its strength, you require just a little for the framing, which adds the amount of light passing on to the plants.

Steel is also very heavy and ensures the greenhouse remains solid no matter the weather conditions or temperature levels. However, the transportation and assembling of the greenhouse can be difficult since the steel is heavy.

Plastic Resin

These are very attractive and are very popular. This is because, compared to aluminum, they are less expensive, and they also do not conduct any heat away from the greenhouse as steel does.

Unfortunately, they lack the strength of the metal frames, and can only be used for the smaller greenhouses, with shorter dimensions. They can only be used with polycarbonate panels.

Wood

Wooden frames are ideal for a simple Do-It-Yourself greenhouse project. Wood is beautiful in appearance and provides sufficient durability and strength but it is susceptible to rotting, therefore does not allow contact with moisture.

Glazing

Tempered Glass

These are strong and impact-resistant. This means that they will withstand any expansions or contractions during the seasonal temperature changes. The 3 mm. single pane thickness is ideal for the greenhouse.

However, the 4 mm. thickness is much stronger and will provide additional insulation. You must protect the hedges during insulation, as the glass may shatter if hit hard. Tempered glass is much more expensive compared to polycarbonate panels.

Tempered glass is more durable even if it is expensive, and it is more resistant to scratches, as well as being very clear and providing no diffusion.

Fiberglass

This is translucent and provides a light that is well-diffused. Fiberglass retains heat better than normal glass. The greenhouses made from fiberglass are normally corrugated to provide adequate rigidity because the outer coat will become sunbaked within 6–10 years. The surface will become etched and yellow.

Polycarbonate

It is UV-treated, lightweight, and durable. It is a high-quality and modern material used for greenhouses. The polycarbonate is available in different levels of thickness and provides the clarity of glass, but it is not scratch resistant, or as strong as tempered glass.

The single-walled one does not retain any heat and provides no light diffusion. It, however, has a longer lifespan of more than 15 years, depending on the region.

Twin-Walled Polycarbonate

This is very popular because it has internal spaces providing strength and excellent insulation. The best point to note about the twin-walled polycarbonate is that it diffuses light.

Triple-Walled Polycarbonate

This is similar to twin-walled polycarbonate, but it has extra strength and heat retention abilities. In cold climates, the triple-walled polycarbonate is extremely useful for all-year-round indoor gardening, because it will withstand snow loads and will freeze without cracking or distorting.

Wind Securities

Any surface such as a wall, fence, or even nearby buildings can act as protection against gusts of wind or even snow. When plants are close to these surfaces, they can leech onto the small amount of warmth that they provide. During summer, if your plants cannot stand the heat, you can use these surfaces as sunblock.

CHAPTER 9.

The Greenhouse Equipment

Digging Tools

Shovel/Spade

I always recommend having a shovel or a spade. These are versatile tools that allow you to work with your soil comfortably. If you head over to the local store, you may find a wide assortment of shovels, each with its own unique design and uses. However, generally speaking, you can use two main types of tools for digging: shovel and spades.

You might find people interchanging the names of shovel and spade to refer to the same tool. However, there is a noticeable difference between a shovel and a spade. And it all comes down to their shape.

If the tool has a round edge, then you are looking at a shovel. With the rounded tip, you can dig into the soil easily. I would suggest that you get a shovel that has a dish able to hold enough dirt.

If you notice that your tool has square edges, then you are looking at a spade. You can use this tool for lifting and throwing aside materials with relative ease. You can also use a spade to pat down the soil after distributing manure. This evens out the soil layer for you.

The type of tool you might require depends on how you plan to work in your garden.

Trowel

Think of this tool as a mini spade. You might have seen this used in construction whenever there is a requirement for spreading cement or mortar. It has a similar purpose in gardening. Essentially, you can use the trowel for flattening soil and giving it an even layer. Additionally, you can dig up materials that you cannot otherwise with a shovel.

That does not mean that a shovel does not have enough strength to lift or break materials. It just means that sometimes, a shovel or a spade has a far reach. With that reach, you might not be able to make small adjustments to your garden wherever required.

Forks

No, not the ones you use to scoop up spaghetti. We are talking about garden forks. While it is not typically used in a garden, its use in digging tasks makes it a must-have in your greenhouse. What you cannot accomplish with a shovel and spade, you can with the garden fork. You simply have to hit this tool into the soil and using the handle's pullback mechanism to easily loosen the soil. This becomes useful when you are trying to remove crops.

Cultivating Tools

When someone mentions the word cultivating, most people imagine a large farmland with a tractor and perhaps some cows. There is a connection there, so you are not entirely wrong. However, cultivating refers to the act of fertilizing the soil and removing any unnecessary weeds.

As you can see, this is an important role and requires the right tool to make it easier for you to get the cultivation done properly.

Hoes

As with all tools, you can get your hands on a variety of hoes. The options might befuddle you, but you just have to remember one essential criterion to having the right hoe: get one that allows you to both pull and push. Apart from that, do note some of the below tips to point you in the direction of the right kind:

- You are not looking for a lightweight tool. Despite what some products might boast about (they are so light, it is like a feather), go for one that is sturdy and strong. This is because you are probably going to be using a lot of effort while working with these tools. You do not want to get one that might break easily.

- Next, you are also looking to get a sharp one. When you push the tool, it has to cut into the soil easily.

Weeder

For those annoying weeds that never seem to go away, you now have a weapon of choice! Often, you might come across weeds that are hard to remove. With the weeder, you can deal with such weeds one at a time.

As with all tools, you might have no shortage of choice. However, what you should be looking for is a weeder that can work with the plants you are growing. If you are unable to decide, always ask for assistance from an expert or the supplier.

Cutting Tools

It is not always about just getting the sharpest tool in the shed. What you are looking for are tools that help you get specific tasks done. Here are some of the tools that you might require for your garden.

Pruners

You might notice that most gardeners always have pruners with them whenever they step out into a garden. What makes this tool so important?

For one, you can perform numerous tasks including snipping off the stems of plants that you have already harvested, cutting flowers after growing them, trimming plants and shrubs, and more.

When selecting a pruner, you need to look for one that has a comfortable handle. At the same time, you should also make sure that it is lightweight. This is because heavy pruners tend to add pressure to your hands, eventually causing discomfort in the long run.

Additionally, look for pruners that have carbon steel blades. This is for the sake of durability. Other forms of material chip away easily and you might find yourself bringing in a whetstone to sharpen the blade.

Check out the safety mechanisms of the pruner. A poor quality one might have weak springs. With weak springs, you might find yourself struggling as the spring cannot hold the pivot together. This causes the pruner to provide resistance, which makes using the tool rather uncomfortable.

Hedge Shears

Another marvelous tool for you to have. Essentially, you are looking at a giant scissor-like object. They are used for cutting items and materials that you might not be able to otherwise cut using a pruner (since they are quite small, after all).

When you are looking for a hedge shear, make sure that you are looking for one that has a cushioned grip. If you have seen a shear in action, then you know that people use both hands, one on each handle provided, to work with the tool. You need something comfortable enough to not add unnecessary pressure on your palms.

The blade itself has to be long and sharp. There is no point in getting short-bladed hedge shears. You might as well save the money and make use of the pruner.

Lopper

Visually, a lopper is like the older, and taller, brother of the pruner. While the blades of both the pruner and the lopper have more or less the same dimensions, the handle is where the difference can be noticed. In a lopper, the handle is longer. This allows you to get into hard-to-reach places.

When looking for a lopper, make sure you get a sturdy handle preferably made out of hardwood or steel. You should also look for rubber handles that allow you a firm and comfortable grip.

Pruning Saw

Finally, when you need to get rid of stubborn stems or weeds that need more than just clippings from pruners, shears, or loppers, then you have the pruning saw.

A lot of people actually end up borrowing a pruning saw from someone else. I do not recommend it. Firstly, the tool itself is not expensive, so you are better off getting a new one. Secondly, you need a pruning saw that is ideal for your garden, so do not look for replacements. Finally, the quality that you get from tools that are borrowed is questionable at best.

CHAPTER 10.

Greenhouse Irrigation Systems

Different Irrigation Systems in Greenhouses

Your greenhouse may have the best climate control system and a rich mix of rot for each plant, but your irrigation system is one of the most important elements for growing flowers, leaves, plants, and healthy fruits. Although you can get away with manual watering with a well of water, using the right method of greenhouse irrigation saves time. The effectiveness of each method depends on the size of the greenhouse.

The system of irrigation for the crop greenhouse includes the following:

1. Manual Watering

This is the most common sprinkler system, but less expensive and more exhausting, but still used when on hand—with labor it is inexpensive and the scale of operation is quite small and automation is not practical. Hand water requires considerable time and is not a pleasant job. But it is always followed when crops are of high density, such as the production of food, shrimp, or pot.

When manual irrigation is practiced, care should be taken to ensure that the strength of the water dissociates, either by using a fine-rose spray or by grinding at the end of the pipe, to avoid washing the root substrate with jars or curves and interrupting the root structure.

2. Perimeter Irrigation System

In this system, the pipes cross the perimeters of a bank with an object that squeezes the surface of the water root under the foliage. Therefore, this system is most relevant for the production of fresh flowers. The tubes can be galvanized iron or PVC can be fixed. In these pipes, the nozzles are mounted at an angle of 45, 90, or 180 degrees. Normally, 19 mm. diameter tubes are used. Depending on the length of the beds, a valve can be supplied later.

3. Tube Sprinkler System

This system is mainly used for water jars. The polyethylene microtube carries water to each pot. These microtubes are available in various internal diameters ranging from 0.9, 1.1, 1.3, 1.5, 1.9 mm., and more.

The number of jars that can be irrigated by a 19 mm main water pipe depends on the internal diameter of the microtube used. For example, a 0.9, 1.1, 1.3, or 1.5 mm. microtube can process 600, 900, 700, and 400 vessels, respectively. These microtubes will have to weigh at the end so that the speed of the water can break, otherwise, the pipe could be blown out of the well and dig a small hole in the media.

4. Drip Irrigation System

This system is ideal for greenhouse cultivation. There is a water-saving of 50–70% compared to the conventional irrigation system. It allows the even distribution of water, nutrients, pesticides, and fungicides without waste.

The drip irrigation system supplies water to crops through a network of main, secondary, and lateral lines with an emission point spaced at regular intervals over the long term. Each diver or transmitter provides a uniform, measured, and controlled application of water, nutrients, pesticides, fungicides, and growth substances directly into the root zone of the plant.

Water and nutrients enter the earth through emitters that move toward the root zone of plants under the combined effect of gravity and capillary forces. In this way, plants immediately acquire moisture and nutrients, which guarantees that plants never suffer from water stress, thus improving their quality. It results in excellent growth and high efficiency.

PVC pipes are used for the distribution of water from the main source to the underlines. Drops from 12–16 mm. droplets are securely placed in each row of plants directly connected to the underlines. The emitters installed in the flanges are located just next to the plant for a gradual distribution of water to the root of the plants.

Pipes should be maintained regularly by adding chlorine or other chemicals to the drift tube to kill bacteria and algae. Acid treatment is also needed to dissolve calcium carbonate. Precautions should be taken against rodents to avoid damaging pipes. Look carefully for leakage hoses, which should be done regularly.

5. Height Spray System

Greenhouse crops are the easiest and least expensive crops that can be irrigated from above. In this system, the tubes are suspended from the floor from 60–180 cm. The nuts are mounted in the tubes at 360°. It will ensure that the water is of good quality and is properly filtered so that these nuts do not get wet.

6. Flow and Reflux System

This is a secondary irrigation system for plant plants and beds. The pots or dishes are grown on a plastic or glass level bench available in different widths (1.2–2.0 m.) and whose length is 1 m. These banks are glued together to form a bank of the desired width. These banks can go for support. These have channels for draining irrigation water.

There is a water tank under the bank. This tank is covered to prevent the growth of dust or algae. For water from the well, the water stays in the bank for 10 minutes and is collected in a cistern and reused. Fertilizers can also be applied through this irrigation system. The pin with the bottom arm is better than the side holes.

Advantages of the Greenhouse Irrigation System

All modern irrigation systems are useful in different ways, depending on their use. Here are some of the reasons why you should consider installing a greenhouse irrigation system:

Filtration Systems

Most greenhouse irrigation systems use filters to prevent the flow path encroachment of small emitters from small particles suspended in the water. New technologies are introduced to reduce obstruction. Some domestic systems are introduced without additional filters because the drinking water is already filtered into the water treatment plant.

Almost all greenhouse equipment companies suggest using filters in a system. Due to sediment collapse and accidental insertion of particles into intermediate tubes, it is advisable to use the latest pipe filters just before the last discharge pipe, in addition to the other filters in the pipe.

Water Conservation

Greenhouse irrigation can guarantee water conservation by reducing evaporation and deep drainage compared to different irrigation methods, such as flood irrigation, because water can be applied, more precisely at the roots of plants.

Besides, the drop can eliminate many diseases that spread by contact with the foliage. In areas where groundwater is limited, there may not be real water savings, but in desert areas or in sandy soils, the system will provide drop irrigation flows.

Factors of Work and Efficiency

Drip irrigation works by water moving slowly and directly to the root of the plant. Just apply water where needed. For example, at the roots of the plant instead of everywhere. Drip systems are simple and relatively insensitive to design and installation errors.

It is a very effective method for water plants. For example, the standard sprinkler system has an efficiency of about 75–85%. In contrast, a greenhouse irrigation system has an efficiency level of more than 90%. But over time, this difference in terms of water supply and efficiency will make a real difference in terms of quality and profitability of the plant.

As expected, in areas where water resources are scarce, such as desert areas around the world, the greenhouse irrigation system has become the preferred method of irrigation.

Irrigation systems are essential in modern agriculture because they greatly improve agricultural production. A greenhouse irrigation system may seem expensive in the short term, but it will save money and effort in the long run. For example, this system can contribute to reducing the cost of production by at least 30% by controlling the amount of water, agrochemicals, and labor costs to implement. However, it is advisable to have a quality greenhouse irrigation system that offers significant benefits.

Grow Stronger Plants With a Good Greenhouse Watering System

There are many different types of greenhouse irrigation systems, but the most common system is the micro irrigation method or more commonly called a drip irrigation system. Tests have shown that using an irrigation system properly can improve plant growth by up to 70%.

Watering the plants is a mistake much make because it is really difficult to judge how much water the plants need. Plants can cause them to rot over-irrigation, get fungal infections, and die. Similarly, underwater it is very easy to dry out the soil and wilt the plants. I do suggest that you invest in a watering system once you have built your greenhouse. And better still, while it is being installed, because at this point it is much easier to install the pipework than later.

Low maintenance extremely handy is a strong irrigation system. You will not have to walk twice a day down to the greenhouse to do the watering. A proper system, designed properly, will provide you with very little maintenance and maintenance for many years of service. Drip irrigation slowly affects the roots of your plants and vegetables with a flow of water. There is very little waste or evaporation as the water gets straight to the soil's roots. This is suitable regardless of the climate in which you are, as you do not need to consider sun and wind evaporation.

Improve Plant Production and Efficiency

The most common practice for small greenhouses is to water the greenhouse by hand. If you have a bigger greenhouse or are interested in taking a more professional approach, I would recommend that you get an automated system. This is an ideal way to increase your production and maintain an efficient business. In the long run, this will not only save you time, but you will also save money.

You may think that hand watering is a low-cost alternative to paying for automated equipment. Yet our experiments have shown that watering plants correctly and uniformly recover the price of equipment. You can never be sure when watering by hand, which plants were overlooked, and which plants were saturated. It is easy to avoid the price of replacing damaged plants by automating the cycle from the start.

Offset Labor Costs

If you are running a growing professional business or perhaps thinking about starting one up, then you have to consider the labor costs. An effective greenhouse watering system is relatively easy to install and will cost much less to operate than the amount you will have to shell out for a season in labor. Prices will vary depending on the region size and the variety of plants being cultivated. Many plants will need more regular watering. Some of them are less common, but with more water. If you water hanging baskets or containers of small size, the best choice is to drip irrigation. When you deal with larger containers, however, it might be worth looking like an option into a spray device.

Chapter 11.

Start Growing in Your Greenhouse

One of the biggest benefits of a greenhouse is it gives you somewhere to start your seedlings off, so you get a head start on the growing season. I always used to start mine on windowsills, but my wife never appreciated me moving the ornaments and family photos to do so. Not to mention that the cats would sit on them, eat them, or just knock them off and get soil on the carpet.

Even a small, plastic portable greenhouse out in your garden is sufficient to start your seeds off, and the extra warmth means you can get a really good head start on the year.

Germinating seeds is something many of us will do every year, but it is often touched and go as to whether or not they will germinate. It can be hard to find enough space to germinate all the seeds that you want to plant, and you end up not planting some crops you wanted to grow.

A greenhouse is a real boon because it gives you plenty of space to start your seeds in a protected environment.

Seed trays and containers are good to get, and I often use ones with plastic lids. This way I can have a greenhouse within a greenhouse or I can use the plastic lid as I am hardening off the seedlings.

There are a huge variety of seed trays on the market, and I use a combination of open trays and trays with cells. Depending on what I am growing I will use different seed trays. Larger cell trays are used for larger plants whereas open trays are used for seeds that can be scattered like beetroot, carrot, and so on.

For some seeds, such as sweetcorn, cardboard tubes (such as those found inside toilet rolls) are good to use because the seedlings do not like being handled. The tubes can be planted straight in the ground, and the cardboard will rot as the seedling grows.

Larger plants such as squashes are best sown in individual pots so they can grow to a decent size without having to be re-potted, which they can object to.

You can use peat pots to grow your seedlings in though I have found these have a habit of either drying out too much or becoming sodden and then rotting. Some people like these but I'm not keen on them.

All of these can be sat in seed trays to make it easier for you to organize your plants. Just remember that you have to pick out your seedlings and re-pot them when they get to a certain size and certain types of plants will not appreciate this.

Heat mats can be used to help with germination, but they are not necessary. If you live in a really cold climate, then they are a benefit, but it does require that you have electricity in your greenhouse, which not everyone will have. You also have the expense of buying the heat mats so you may get 1–2 to start off your most important or delicate seedlings.

I have a hydroponic system with grow lamps at home which I use to start off seedlings like tomatoes and pumpkins. These are then transplanted to pots and put in the greenhouse where they continue to flourish.

You need to think about the light requirements of each plant because some seedlings prefer more light to others. More sun-sensitive seedlings will need shading from the heat of the midday sun.

One useful technique when sowing seeds in individual pots is to place 2–3 seeds into each pot, spaced out evenly. This way if 1–2 seeds do not germinate you still have a 3rd that could grow. If all 3 grow, then you can either prick out and re-plant the 3 seedlings, or you can discard the smaller seedlings, keeping the strongest.

All seeds need to be covered by the growing medium but not too deeply otherwise they will not push through the soil to the light. Check the packets to determine exactly how deeply to plant each seed.

For bigger seeds, it is easy to poke them into the soil. One thing to remember with larger seeds, such as squash seeds, is to plant them on their sides so they can grow the right way up. If they are put in the ground the wrong way, then you can find the roots coming up through the soil and the leaves growing underground! This often happens when children help with the planting.

For smaller seeds, you need to cover them with a sprinkling of soil to stop them from blowing away. With smaller seeds, you will need to be careful watering them as they can float away with excess water!

Seeds can take anything from a few days to a few weeks to germinate, depending on the type of plant you are growing. Check the packet for specific timings, so you know when to start checking your seedlings.

During this time, you need to keep them moist, but not wet otherwise the seeds can rot. Check the pots regularly and make sure they are not too damp. Peat pots can go moldy if the humidity is too high so you need to keep an eye on them too. Remember that with a greenhouse you can start your seedlings earlier in cooler areas than you can outside.

Hardening Off

Not all of your seedlings are going to spend their lives in your greenhouse; some will be planted outside. Moving a plant from the protective enclosure that is your greenhouse into the great outdoors can be an incredible shock to the system. The difference in environments causes shock which can at best stunt the growth of your plant by several weeks, and at worst kill it!

Hardening off your seedlings is vital if you want them to survive and thrive when you plant them outside of your greenhouse. You will be surprised how many people do not do this and struggle to get their plants to grow.

The process of hardening off is not done overnight and can take 1–2 weeks, depending on the weather where you live. You will have to be patient, but it is worth it as it strengthens your plants and ensures they grow well.

Once there is no risk of frost during the day you take your seedlings out of your greenhouse and leave them outside during the day. Put them somewhere that is warm but not too sunny, and that is sheltered from the wind.

Leave your seedlings outside for most of the day and then mid to late afternoon move them back into your greenhouse.

Should your plants show any sign of stress such as browning, wilting, or yellowing then move the hardening process back a step and try again the following day.

Water well during this process and then after the 2 weeks, you should be able to plant your seedlings out in the ground.

Sorting Your Seed Packets

Most gardeners will have seed packets pretty much everywhere, in drawers, on shelves, tucked away in cupboards. They accumulate, and it is far too easy to get overwhelmed by them. You know what it is like, you get halfway through the growing season and realize you forgot to plant something because you could not find the seeds!

There are plenty of different ways for you to organize your seed packets and it is up to you how best you do it.

Firstly, I sort the seeds into 3 piles:

1. Herbs.

2. Flowers.

3. Vegetables.

These are stored separately.

Each seed packet is filed under the first month in which it can be planted.

For me, this is the best way to organize my seeds because I know that in January, I can look at my January seeds and decide what to plant (assuming I do not have a plan for the year). It makes my life much easier because I am not sorting through piles of seeds trying to work out what I should be planting.

This is my method and it works very well for me. It keeps me a little bit more organized and saves time when it comes to deciding what to plant.

If you find a different system that works for you, then by all means use that.

Remember that if a seed packet states it can be planted out in a month, then you can often start the seedling off in a greenhouse between 4-8 weeks earlier, depending on whether it is heated or not!

A greenhouse is a real boon when it comes to starting off seedlings and will help you get a head start on the growing season. It also gets the seed trays out of the house and gives your plants a great start in life.

Many growers tend to ask about the difference between vegetables, herbs, and fruits. On one hand, vegetables are any edible part of a plant and can be eaten either raw or cook; it does not have any seeds. Herbs, on the other hand, refer to plants or part of plants that are grown as food and also for medicinal purpose while fruits are eatable products containing seeds which are formed from the matured ovary of a flowering plant. The major difference is that while fruits can be referred to as vegetables, vegetables cannot exactly be termed fruits. Also, it is arguable that not all herbs are eaten as the main ingredient as is the case with vegetables.

Growing Vegetables in a Greenhouse

Vegetables are suitable plants to cultivate in a greenhouse because the demand for them is usually high all through the year. However, the vegetables require the right environmental condition for successful cultivation. The grow lights in the greenhouse should be energy efficient and cover the vegetable plantation. During the cold season, the best vegetables to cultivate include tomatoes, lettuce, spinach, peppers, and cucumbers. But with experience, any kind of vegetable can be successfully cultivated when provided with the right temperature. The key is to maintain a nighttime temperature between 40–62ºF in the greenhouse depending on the type of vegetable. One of the major issues growers face when it comes to growing vegetables in a greenhouse is the issue of pollination. While some vegetables, like tomatoes and peppers, can self-pollinate, the others that cannot self-pollinate will require hand pollination. This is achieved by taking the anther of a vegetable and rubbing it carefully against the stigma of another vegetable for a successful transfer of pollen grains. Sometimes, the vegetables that can self-pollinate require being shaken to successfully pollinate but a circulation fan can be installed for this purpose.

Vegetables need water but not too much and so it is important not to overwater your greenhouse vegetable garden. A good ventilation system in place will maintain the proper humidity level which will aid the growth of the vegetables in the greenhouse. Using air conditioners in your greenhouse is not the best practice because what conditioners actually do is reduce the moisture content in the growing environment. It is advisable to use evaporative air coolers in the greenhouse instead.

CHAPTER 12.

Planting in Warm and Cold Weather

Cold Weather

While having a greenhouse will provide you the opportunity to grow the so-called winter plants effectively, it is no guarantee that you will be able to raise them well. You will still need to equip yourself with the right techniques for raising plants in cold weather. Next are some tips that can help you get by, as well as some plants that are best suited for such weather conditions.

Growing cold-weather plants during the winter seasons allows you to make very minimal adjustments to the conditions inside your greenhouse. Oftentimes, the minimal amount of sunlight received during these cold periods is more than enough to provide heat sufficient enough for these plants to survive. In fact, subjecting them to summer-type temperatures can prove detrimental to their growth. Another advantage of planting cold-weather plants during this season is the fact that they can withstand even occasional freezing temperatures.

You can grow these plants in low-temperature, low-light conditions without encountering too many problems. Among the staples of cold weather, growing include leafy plants such as cabbage, lettuce, and spinach. Cruciferous vegetables such as broccoli and cauliflower also thrive in such conditions. Also, plants that grow massive roots such as beets and carrots are known to be cold-weather plants. Other plants that are known to thrive during this time of the year include peas, radishes, turnips, green onions, chard, and kohlrabi.

A lot of these plants are capable of growing with minimal supervision and without any special treatment. Of course, you got to make sure that you provide your plants with sufficient care at all times. To ensure that your plants would grow accordingly, here are some tips that can prove useful:

- **Avoid extreme temperature:** While cold-weather plants are resilient to temperature changes, it is not advisable to expose these plants to either extreme cold or heat. Make sure to not make your greenhouse either too hot or too cold. As these plants are more used to cool weather, too much heat would not be conducive for their growth. As a final reminder, it is not healthy for the plant to be subjected to temperature fluctuations as it is a source of stress for them.

- **Keep the light flowing:** Getting light is a bit tricky especially during the winter season. As days are shorter during the cold months, you will need to make the most out of the sunlight that comes in. However, you might need to supplement some light thru your built-in lighting system. This is especially so for seedlings still at the nursery. In fact, some seeds do not sprout without enough light. As a guide, study the photoperiod of the specific plant you are intending to cultivate.

Warm Weather

While some people think that the greenhouse is only designed for cold-weather planting, it is actually designed to be used for any weather condition. Gardening is fun to do during the months of spring and summer, so why should you hold back from growing your favorite plants? As long as you know the right skills, and here are some tips that can help you grow plants in your greenhouse during warm weather as well as which plants are great to grow during this season.

Usually, you grow plants outdoors during the warm season. However, growing indoors offers more potential for growth than giving some extra hours of sunlight. It saves you from contending with all other factors that may cause problems for you and your plants. This is the time when you will have to plant warm-weather plants. The relatively high temperatures combined with the direct and uninterrupted supply of sunlight will make these plants flourish. They also thrive during nights when the temperature is moderately warm.

Numerous plants flourish during warm weather. Fruit-bearing plants such as watermelon, melon, squash, and tomatoes all thrive in situations when both light and warmth are in a constant supply. Tropical plants such as citrus plants, peppers, eggplant, and cucumber also grow prominently under these conditions. Other popular plants such as beans and berries also thrive under these conditions. As long as you get to know about the needs of each individual plant, you should not have too much problem raising warm-weather plants inside a greenhouse.

Planting in warm weather may seem like a walk in the park, but there is absolutely no room for complacency here. Just like in cold weather, things can go wrong even when there is sufficient sunlight around. Here are some tips that can guide you when raising plants in warm weather:

- **Be careful of too much heat and humidity:** While these so-called warm weather plants are adept at surviving in warm environments, there is always such a thing as too much warmth. When the weather gets too hot, your plants will literally wilt. In fact, it has been estimated that most garden plants can only tolerate up to 90–100°F at most. When it gets hot, you will need to make use of temperature management systems such as fans and vents. You can also control the humidity inside your greenhouse.

- **Water your plants wisely:** Watering your plants is a crucial element of taking care of plants during the spring and summer. The amount of water needed by a specific plant is generally dependent on its individual needs. Other than making sure that their needs are satisfied, you also got to watch out for creating too much humidity. Because of this, it is generally recommended that you water your plants twice a day: during the middle of noon and the night.

CHAPTER 13.

Year-Round Growing

When you plant your plants in a greenhouse, you can allow them to give you harvest as often as you want to. Obviously, plants will only give you a harvest when they are ready to. However, with the process of growing your plants on a schedule, you can make sure that you have some sort of harvest coming in all year long. We will look into how this works and some tips and tricks to help you along the way.

First, let's look into why you would want to have a harvest all year long. If you have plants that can be harvested all year long, you have fresh fruits and vegetables available to you every day of the year. If you grow enough plants, this could even replace your produce purchases at the grocery store. It will allow your family and yourself to be the healthiest versions of yourself that you can possibly be. It will give you something to look forward to each day, and it will allow you to continue to feel the success of growing in your greenhouse throughout every single season. Having a year-round harvest greenhouse can be a challenging process, and we will look into these struggles below along with the benefits— but it can be a great thing as well.

Next, let's look into how you can make this happen. How can you possibly have a greenhouse that has products available to you every single day of the year? It sounds like something that would be fairly difficult. In reality, it is actually a simple process. It requires a lot of work and a lot of planning, but once you get that plan into action, it can be a simple thing to follow through with.

To learn about how you can make this happen, let us look into what we already know. We already know that you can plant in greenhouses all year long. We already know that you can keep your plants alive in your greenhouse all year long and that you do not need to keep planting new plants for each season. Your plants can stay alive. We know that this is possible through the use of heaters and adequate lighting through artificial sources when it is winter, and we know that this is possible through fans and vents when it is hot in the summer. When you have a greenhouse that can be used every season of the year, you can, of course, plant in every season of the year.

Now, let's look into what we do not yet know. We do not yet know how you can have plants give you a crop all year long. Of course, you are not going to get a tomato plant to keep producing your tomatoes constantly day after day for years straight. Fruits and vegetables have growing seasons. They have seasons where they grow food and they have seasons where they prepare themselves to do so. You cannot make an apple tree have apples all year long. You cannot make an orange tree grow oranges all year long. The plants need to have their time to prepare themselves, they cannot have food on them every single day.

Because of this, there must be another way to allow you to gain a crop from your greenhouse every day of the year. This other way is by planting your plants on the schedule. When you plant a seed, you know when it will become mature by the number of days it provides you on the back of the packet. For example, if a tomato plant takes 120 days to reach maturity, this will be listed on the back of the seed packet. When you know how long it will take to produce fruit or vegetables, you will be able to count on that plant to produce a crop for you at that time. Because of this, you will then know if you plant a tomato plant that you will have tomatoes in 120 or so days. The same holds true for every type of plant. When you plant something, you should be able to tell how long it will take that seedling to turn into a plant that bears food.

Now, if you want to have every month of the year filled with these tomatoes, you will need to plan a harvest for each month of the year. Once you count back these 120 days, you will find the day that you need to plant your seed on. On Columbus Day, you will probably want to plant many seeds. If you plant many seeds, you will have a better chance of getting at least some of them to survive. As we mentioned earlier in the book, not all seeds will turn into seedlings. Because of this, you will want to plant many seeds to ensure that you get some plants out of your effort.

After you have planted your seeds, go ahead and find the next date when you would like a new tomato harvest to happen and do the process all over again. If you want your harvest to happen once a month, you can simply plant the seeds on the first day of every month. Once you have gotten the pattern started, the math will always be 30 days later. Because of this, you can simply plant on one day of the month every month.

If you plant one day of the month every month for a year, you should then have a harvest coming in every single day of the year. As long as you care for your plants in a way that allows them to bear fruit and vegetables, will have your plants set up on a staggering schedule to give you a crop.

You can choose to do this year-round growing with one type of plant or with all of your plants. If you only want carrots year-round, for example, you could simply just choose to keep planting carrot seeds when you want them to grow. If you only have a small greenhouse, you can consider only doing year-round growing with your favorite plants.

If you live in a cold area, you will want to make sure that your greenhouse is winterized and ready for the cold winter. You will want to make sure that your heater is working and that it is running, as well as that all cracks and holes that could be in your greenhouse are covered and are not letting air in. You will also want to make sure that any big jobs are done before winter comes so that you do not have to open the doors or windows for long amounts of time as this can make the air in the greenhouse become very cold very quickly. If you are growing year-round and you live in a place that has very hot summers, you may want to be prepared with things like some shades and vents on your greenhouse for air circulation. For the spring and fall, you need to be prepared as well. The preparation for these seasons varies based on where you live—but for the fall, you should basically be prepared for winter; and for the spring, you should be basically prepared for summer.

Why do you need to have your greenhouse ready for every season? You need to have your greenhouse ready for every season because you are growing in every season. If you have a harvest every day, that means you are growing every day. This means that your plants need to be alive and healthy every day. To make this happen, your greenhouse needs to be repaired and in the optimal environment for the health of your plants as well as their success every day of the year. It has a much more detailed approach to this information.

Another thing to consider when you look into year-round growing is that you need to be ready to do a lot of work every single day of the year. When you do year-round growing, you do not have an off-season. You do not have a break in between crops where you do not need to go out into your greenhouse. You do not have a time where you are not doing multiple jobs at once. You are actually growing seedlings, planting seeds, caring for plants, and harvesting all on the same day. This means that year-round growing can take a lot of your time and energy in ways that typical greenhouse gardening cannot. Of course, this extra effort does provide a lot of added benefits with its increased amount of crop and harvest, but it needs to be a level of work that you are ready for if it is something that you want to consider. This extra work also takes up a lot of extra time. If you want to have a year-round growing garden inside of your greenhouse, you need to make sure that you have enough time to do so. Finding the time to prep for each season, plant seeds, care for your plants, and harvest all at the same time can be really challenging. Year-round growing inside of your greenhouse is a commitment that you really need to be all in for if you want even to consider it.

With extra harvests, year-round growing also comes with extra costs. If you want to grow plants year-round, you will be buying many more seeds. You will also be buying much more soil, and maybe even many more trays if you cannot reuse the old ones. You will be using more water in your extra plants, and you will be using lighter to provide the heat and lighting that your extra plants need. Make sure that you can cover these extra costs if you are ready to have extra harvests year-round growing in your greenhouse.

Another thing that you should know about year-round gardening is it is great for people who want to sell their crops. If you are looking to sell fruits or vegetables, year-round gardening can be a great choice. If you do your own gardening and sell your crops, you will be one of the few farmers or gardeners who can sell fruits and vegetables during their offseason. If you can sell fruits and vegetables during their offseason, you will have a huge advantage over your competition. Typically, people really miss fresh fruits and vegetables in the wintertime. You will have a lot of happy customers, and the extra work that you put into your year-round gardening will pay off quickly.

Year-round growing can be hard. Because of this, we want to share with you some pieces of advice. Let's look into some tips and tricks that you can use to make year-round growing easier for you:

- Our first step is that you should start with a plan. Make sure that you know what you want to do. If you do not have a plan in place before you begin, year-round growing can seem really overwhelming. You need to know what types of plants you want to have and when you want to harvest them. You also want to have a plan for where you are going to grow your plants since they take up extra space as well as how you are going to get the extra resources. You may even want to plan out how you are going to have enough time to spend growing all of these plants at once.

- It is okay if you have a small greenhouse, but if you do have a small greenhouse, you need to be creative with the small space that you have. Look into different shelving units, or even considered growing one set the plants underneath the normal bench with artificial grow lights to maximize your space.

- Ask your neighborhood children to help you with planting seeds. These are things that your family, friends, and neighbors would probably love to help you with if you asked him. The extra help would also give you the ability to care for plants in a way that you may not be able to do on your own.

- Along with that last tip, if you offer some of the harvests to your helpers, they may be much more willing to help. Tell your neighbors that they can take some tomatoes whenever they like if they come over and help water them or help you plant some seeds. If you spread the word that your helpers will get it back in produce that comes from your garden, you will probably have many more volunteers as well as much better luck getting them actually to come and help.

- Our biggest tip for year-round growing is to be prepared. Look ahead at the challenges that you might face. Be ready for what you need to do if you have some sort of greenhouse emergency. Make sure that you understand you will be using many more lights and much more water. Understand that you will be spending a lot of time in the greenhouse. Make yourself comfortable with these facts and even happy with them. If you do these things, it will be much easier for you to grow your plants year-round in a greenhouse.

Even though growing plants year-round in a greenhouse is hard, we want you to find success. We believe that if you follow these tips and tricks and learn all the information that we have shared with you, you will be able to have success at year-round gardening.

Overall, it is easy to see that year-round growing inside of a greenhouse is a difficult but rewarding task. It is something that takes extra time, extra money, extra resources, extra effort, and extra dedication to keep up with it. Along with all of these things, however, year-round growing in a greenhouse also provides you with added benefits. It gives you harvests year-round. It allows you to have healthy food to put on your table every day of the year. It allows you to plan for what you want to eat and when you want to have it ready. It is a rewarding and beneficial process in many ways. Year-round growing can be a great thing to do—you just need to make sure that you are up for the challenge before you begin.

CHAPTER 14.

Managing a Greenhouse, Pest, and Disease

Pest Control—Managing Pests

The term pest control often conjures up images of people using sprays filled with chemicals. You might think that using such methods is rather extreme. But if you spot your wonderful tomatoes surrounded by ants or your beautiful flowers suddenly attacked by flies, then you might think of drowning those creatures in pesticides.

However, what might sound like a frightening scenario can typically be solved by taking a few precautionary steps.

The thing about pesticides is that they have an instant (and noticeable) effect. You can see the number of pests on your plants reduced. Nevertheless, there are certain effects in the long term—such as depleting the health of your soil and slightly poisoning your water—that might prove disastrous for you in the future. You might have to change the soil entirely. If you are using a raised bed, then this might not be a problem. However, if you have decided to plant directly into the earth, then getting rid of all that pesticide residue is a strenuous process.

Here is another thing that you should keep in mind; sometimes, getting rid of the pests may not be necessary. If you have aphids roaming around on your plants, then see if you have helpful insects that dine on these aphids. In fact, certain farmers are known to let the pests live. This is because they usually have some form of predator that can take care of the pest problem. This has two beneficial results:

- You do not have to spend time (and money, in some situations) on pest control activities.

- You let someone (or something) else take care of the problem for you.

Another thing to keep in mind; your problem might not be related to pests. It is easy to think that certain creatures have wreaked havoc on your lovely garden. Actually, it is certainly tempting to think that way. However, in many cases, the situation might just be because of other factors. Is there enough moisture for the plants? Are strong winds causing harm to them? Was there heavy rainfall recently? Did it hail? Even water pollution could be another factor to consider. You see, all of these factors cause unnecessary stress on the plants, which further begins to attract the pests in your area. Trying to get to the root of the problem might help you effectively remove the pests without using any pest control techniques (including pesticides).

The idea behind evaluating your garden is to know what kind of problem you are dealing with. That may help you decide if you would like to head over to the next step, which is the integrated pest management, or "IPM" for short, process.

In IPM, farmers and gardeners take gradually stronger steps to get rid of the pests in their garden. They start by working on the conditions that help the growth of the crops. Are these conditions beneficial? Do the crops have everything they need? Once they can work around these conditions, they seek to establish a level of damage they can accept. Once that is done, they move on to using methods that have minimal toxicity. If that does not work, they begin using toxic or invasive methods.

Join the Resistance!

Some of these plants have some unique traits. One of those unique traits is the ability of the plant to have disease resistance. This means that the plant suffers minimal damage from a specific disease, similar to how the human immune system builds resistance against diseases.

Many of the modern plants have built resistance to many diseases that could cause considerable damage. What is more, you can find plants that also have resistance to certain insects. For example, you can find special types of squash that can keep away certain types of beetles. This might help you effectively find a solution against these pests without having to resort to other methods of pest control.

In fact, when you are purchasing plants, you might receive information about what pests those plants resist. After knowing what pests are common in your area, you can match the plant to that particular pest.

Inviting Fewer Pests

While you might be confident that you have taken all the precautionary steps to keep away pests, there might be certain reasons your garden is still attracting those nasty critters.

Plant Conditions

Make sure you have placed the plant in the right spot, based on how much water, sunlight, and essential nutrients that the plant may require. This is because stress begins to affect those plants that do not receive what they require. The stress, in turn, causes plants to release certain chemicals in the air, which are like beacons for all the pests in the area. Humans might deal with stress through many means. Plants, however, do not have mechanisms to resist stress. They eventually begin to experience deteriorating health and finally succumb to the effects of pests. This does not mean that healthy plants cannot attract pests, but they are capable of surviving attacks when an unhealthy plant may not be able to.

Mixed Plants

Most insects have receptors that allow them to target their favorite plants. It is how bees can seek out nectar so easily. If you have the plants that insects are waiting to attack and you have done nothing to protect those plants, then you might as well schedule buffet hours for the insects! What you can do to avoid this situation is to plant your crops in small batches throughout your garden. Then you can add other plants into the mix (preferably those that have resistance against the pests in your area). This confuses the insects, tricking them into believing that perhaps your garden does not have the food they are looking for. Additionally, you might be able to avoid diseases from spreading when you mix plant breeds.

Timing

Certain pests often arrive during certain climates. This fact might give you an idea of the kind of threat you are dealing with. When plants are young, they do not have the strength to ward off pests effectively, which is why you can plant your crops early so that by the time pest climate arrives, your crops have strong tissues. In some cases, insects often leave eggs behind in gardens. When the larvae hatch, they find a ready source of food in the plants around them. For this reason, you could also plant your crops a few weeks after the larvae have hatched, allowing you to starve the pests before working on your garden.

Here is a pro tip: Speak to farmers in your area about the emergence of pests. They have extensive knowledge about when these pests might come out during a particular season, allowing you to know how long to wait before planting your crops.

Crop Rotation

You can move around the crops to new locations in your greenhouse each year. This does not give pests a particular spot to target. Shifting locations confuses the pests, who might be used to finding plants in a specific spot of the garden. Certain insects often lay their eggs in one location when they realize that they know where they can find a ready supply of food. However, by moving your crops around, larvae that hatch might not find their food source. Before they can discover food, they might starve and you might be able to get rid of them without much effort. Do note that crop rotation is most commonly possible with annual plants when they can be cycled year after year. Perennial plants are usually harvested after one year, so they cannot be quickly rotated. So, make a note of this when you plan to change plant locations in your garden.

Common Mistakes and How to Avoid Them

In fact, truth to tell, many gardeners continue to make mistakes despite having acquired years of experience. The most common reason why mistakes are made is ignorance. Some people simply think that if they can raise carrots, then they can raise lettuce, or if they can grow an orange tree, then they understand how to take care of mint. This attitude ignores the subtle (and not so subtle) differences between plants, and simply reduces a vast topic into too rigid a formula. When this happens, dead plants and poor harvests are prone to follow.

By being aware of these mistakes, you reduce your level of ignorance, and you increase your chances of avoiding them yourself. In the world of growing, much as with life in general, we are required to act on our knowledge if we want to see the best results.

Not Doing Your Research

We've looked at a handful of plants throughout this book, and, while some of them share similarities (such as thyme and rosemary), they all have notable differences in how much light, water, fertilizer, space, and humidity they want, as well as which nutrients they like best, and what pH level they require to stay healthy. If there can be this much of a difference between the small handful that we were able to look at, then you can only imagine how much variety there is across the plant kingdom. Not only that, but keep in mind that different subspecies of plants often have their own preferences that, while similar to each other, can show a great deal of variation.

Instead, do your research on your plants. If you are not very technologically savvy, then you should consider stopping in at your local gardening center and asking them for advice. The chances are good, you were going to get your seeds from them anyway, so why not pick their brains first to find out everything you need to know. Questions you should consider asking are: How often should I water this plant? What type of fertilizer do they need and how often do they need it? Does it take long to germinate? How long does it take to grow? When can I expect it to start fruiting? How much light does it want? Does it prefer direct sunlight or partial shade? What temperature should it be kept at? How much humidity does it require? What pH level will it need? Is there anything I should know about pollinating it by hand?

Asking questions and doing your research should be the very first step you take when considering growing something that is new to you. Before you, even lookup the price of seeds or seedlings, ask all the questions you need answering, whether or not you are capable of providing an ideal environment for this type of plant. Being prepared with information will save you money as you can avoid those that are not a good fit, and you will also spare yourself the disappointment of watching a new plant wilt and die.

Growing Too Much at Once

When they are beginning, many people have big, grand plans for their indoor gardens. They are going to have lettuce and tomatoes, carrots and eggplants, a peach tree, some rosemary, and a bunch of mints. In theory, this sounds amazing. Who wouldn't want to have that much delicious food at their fingertips? But in practice, this is often a recipe for disaster.

The first issue that many people are going to run into by expanding too fast is the fact that things are not growing as they thought. Just because you plant a seed, does not mean it is going to grow. It can be particularly discouraging for new gardeners when it happens once but consider when it happens to several plants all at the same time. Furthermore, even if they do germinate, each plant is going to grow at a different rate, and this means that you will need to balance the needs of several different plants that are all at various stages of development. Pay special attention to the use of the word "balance." Gardening takes up your time and attention; you need to watch your plants to get a sense of how they are doing, and then adjust their care accordingly. While you might think that this will be quick and easy, many new gardeners are completely shocked at just how long this can take.

When you are starting, begin small and then expand as you become more comfortable with looking after a garden. While I would suggest starting with a single plant, many will find this to be too small to make it worth their time. If you need more, allow yourself 2–3 plants but limit yourself to this. Pick plants that have similar care routines and environmental requirements so that you can worry about building one environment, rather than fine-tuning several. Take these plants through to harvest before you add any more. That way, you know what is required for each step.

In the care process. Start slow, and add more as your skill and understanding increase. Approach it with a sensible attitude. Looked at this way, becoming proficient at gardening is not that different from any other skill.

Planting Seeds Too Close Together

When you are first putting seeds (or even seedlings) into a container, it will seem like space is abundant. After all, seeds are super-tiny, and so you can put a whole whack of them in a container without it feeling like they are crowding each other out. While this is true at these early stages of growth, you will quickly come to regret this decision when your plants start to grow, and you realize that they have no space at all. But why is this a bad thing, necessarily?

First off, while you will notice the lack of space on top of the soil, it is really what is happening under the soil that is damaging your plants the most. Their roots are going to start to get tangled and fight to find their own space while they grow, and this is going to cause several issues that negatively affect their overall health. Those same roots are going to have to compete with each other for nutrients, and this means that all of your plants are going to be far less healthy when compared to those that get all the nutrients they need without a struggle. The struggle to fight for nutrients wastes energy, energy which would be better utilized in promoting growth. Stunted plants are one such result of being planted too close together.

Another factor to bear in mind is that pests and diseases can much more easily spread from plant to plant when they are too close together. Moreover, they have more places to hide; it is much harder to see all the nooks and crannies of your plants when they obscure each other. Therefore, it is evident that planting too close together creates more difficulties with pests and diseases and smaller harvests of less tasty food.

Not Checking for Pests or Cleaning for Disease

Speaking of pests—have you been checking for them? If not, then how do you know that your plants are still healthy? Just because you do not see pests when you look at your plants does not mean that they might not already be feeding off your plants. There are many telltale signs of infection such as discoloration in leaves, bumps or holes in the leaves, or leaves that have begun to wilt for no discernible reason. The longer an infestation takes hold, the more damage your plants will sustain, and they can only take so much before they give up and die.

You want to ensure your plants are free of infestation or infection; the simplest precaution is to check them daily. This takes up time, that resource many new growers discount when they decide to grow too many plants. While many pests can be detected on sight, there are more than a few that either hide or are invisible to the naked eye. If you see pests, you need to start treating your plants immediately. But you should also do spot tests daily to see if any such parasites are hiding. Use your rake to check the soil at the roots, as many pests lay eggs in the soil; the offspring of these eggs will, given the chance, chew away at the stem. If the paper comes away with streaks of blood, then there are pests you are going to have to deal with. There are many methods of dealing with pests but you should do your research before embarking on any of them. Since fruits, vegetables, and herbs are all plants that we grow with the intention of eating, it is crucial to ensure that whatever pesticide or solution you use to treat your plants is not going to harm the food you eat.

While you are making it a habit to check for pests, you should also keep your eyes open for signs of disease. White powdery mildew, molds, discoloration, wilting branches, rotting fruit—all of these are signs that your plants have caught a disease. The first step in tackling most sicknesses is to cut away any infected parts and immediately dispose of them outdoors. Apply treatments to your plants after ensuring those treatments are not harmful to humans.

Next, check the pH level of the soil to make sure that they have enough nutrients, as too few can leave them sickly, and too many can cause a nutrient burn. Finally, though just as importantly, make sure that dead plant matter is removed from the area. The compost that is used in the soil is fine but leaves or branches that have fallen off the plants and are rotting in the general area are quite harmful. This rotting plant matter, when it is not being used as part of a properly planned feeding system can introduce harmful bacteria to your growing area. Always make sure you remove any dead or fallen plant matter from the growing area and wash your hands first before you start handling your plants.

CHAPTER 15.

Making Money With Your Greenhouse

Everybody wants to make some extra money on the side, and if you are in gardening, you might want to start looking at some commercial greenhouses. We all have to make some extra cash, and what better way to do it than with something that you enjoy. You will note that those who enjoy gardening are the only people who consider making money from growing plants in commercial greenhouses.

If you are looking to enter the industry, you will find that you are going to need more than just your backyard. The key is to start small, but you also want to make sure you get rid of all the pests, and other stuff that will cost you money in damages, and the elements are one of those things. Most avid gardeners know that in summer you cannot grow any trees, plants, vegetables, and fruits and some of them cannot grow in winter.

That is why they are going to look at wide-span greenhouses that allow them to weather exposure. If you have control over a few things, such as the temperature in your garden, you can grow the most beautiful plants that will make you money in the long run. The one thing you need to understand is that going into such a company will not get you to cash instantly.

This is because you need time to grow all you grow, well, to grow. Many things take as little as a few weeks, but you will have to be able to put in the time if you are looking to grow the big-ticket items for sale. This means you will either need to do this on the side, or you will need to have enough money to take you from one growing season to the next.

The great thing about commercial greenhouses is they offer you the gable truss that looks very nice. Most greenhouses are built in the form of a flat roof or a funny triangle; with the commercial ones, you can note that they almost look like barns, which is what so many professionals love.

The other thing you have to say about this is appears to be a little more expensive than the typical gardener, variety. If you are going to get into growing plant life for sale, you will find it is always a good thing to start small, but eventually, you will need to get bigger, and that is going commercial.

You will also note that the commercial greenhouses in architecture and structure are much better than the normal version of the backyard. The shell is made of hard polycarbonate plastic, which helps keep in the heat, and metal poles support the structure. The poles make overhead sprinkler systems and lights easy to install, but if you are trying to get high, you might want to know a little more about drip irrigation.

Successful Greenhouse Is a Great Business Opportunity

What you must know is timing is critical for any product you grow in your profitable greenhouse. The timing should be perfect so that you can get the best products on the market for sampling. You should expect your name to travel quickly if you have the best. You will sell every product that is produced like hot pancakes in no time at all.

It used to be for fun to have and maintain a greenhouse. Not as those who already have one know how to make money from the seeds, fruits, and vegetables that can be created by the greenhouse. People are crying out to them because they know the fruits and vegetables are safe to eat, especially if they know the greenhouse owner. They have an understanding of how they are developed and grown naturally.

The fact is that people want to live well, and there is one way to eat well. So, to start eating better, you should start eating right-grown foods. You can also have fruits and vegetables that are not in season with the greenhouse. So, you can get fruits that you only saw in winter during the season. Neighbors are also going to cry out for it. So be prepared with your profitable greenhouse to make profits.

Save Your Time and Money

You might wonder whether it is worth the effort to create a greenhouse in your backyard. It will be a challenge, especially if you do not have any experience in woodworking or carpentry. You may be better off buying a greenhouse kit from your local garden supply store. You will still need to mount the greenhouse, though. To complete the construction process, you must rely on a set of instructions. Ideally, the directions will be sufficiently detailed to make your greenhouse building a fun one.

If you are up to the greenhouse challenge, it is highly recommended that you adopt some kind of reliable strategy. This greenhouse design should be sufficiently detailed to direct the construction phase step-by-step and help make your greenhouse construction project a success. This plan should outline the order you need to build your greenhouse to avoid wasting your time.

You can ultimately spend more money on materials without a strategy than you ever anticipated. A good plan would tell you exactly what you need to do to get the job done right. At the beginning of your greenhouse project, having the right materials will save you money in the long run.

This plan should also provide you with a list of tools you need to build your greenhouse properly and efficiently. Understanding this will save you time because, from the beginning, you will have all the right tools.

This will help you avoid the need to hunt for solutions in the middle of your project and waste your valuable time.

Such designs should also include other elements of your greenhouse. Such plans should include how your greenhouse's interior should be adequately heated and insulated. Understanding this will enable you to save your greenhouse heating energy.

Getting a Profitable Greenhouse Is Within Your Reach

If you think about it, particularly if you are resourceful, even with the recent global economic crisis, money is not hard to get through. If you just put your mind to it, you can make a lot of money out of anything. More often than not, those with green thumbs who already have greenhouses do not think about turning their hobby into a lucrative one. For them, their greenhouse brings them quiet. It is like having a little world. They are the only ones and their plants. The greenhouse plants and vegetables provided them with warmth, fun, and beauty. Did not they know they could turn it into something big?

When it comes to their hobby, all it takes is to change your way of thinking so you can make a successful greenhouse. Cash is a powerful incentive. Your greenhouse will be able to provide something else besides putting food on the table. Who knows about it? You can now check all the items you have put on your wish list one by one.

CHAPTER 16.

Choosing Your Plants and Running the First Growing Cycle

How to Choose What to Grow in Your Greenhouse?

Whether you are new to greenhouse gardening or you have been there for a couple of years, you need to plan what you want to grow in your greenhouse to suit your needs and lifestyle. Do not worry about this subject, but look at who you are and how you can enjoy small greenhouse gardening while achieving your gardening goals.

The effort is a big factor in effective gardening, and if you have a more casual approach to your garden, then choose plant or vegetable varieties that do not take as long as other plants that need constant attention. On the other hand, you can look forward to a focused effort to grow and abundantly multiple plant species. A little preparation and analysis will quickly give you some ideas about which plant types can be easily grown under similar conditions of soil and light and are consistent with the amount of effort you are willing to put in.

One of my favorite ways to choose which vegetables I want to grow is to look at how I prepare dinner for my family and the food we want. There is nothing like finding all the fresh salad ingredients that were all grown in my greenhouse. I also like the freshly grown vegetables that helped my children take care of and harvest for a pot roast. Maybe you like a salsa garden or herb garden to jazz up some of the dishes you are cooking, so why does not your little greenhouse garden grow those things? One of my favorite vegetables in the garden is fresh, small red potatoes. I enjoy steaming them and then cutting them in half and frying them in butter and garlic, and the only difficulty I have is that my children love them. My whole point is to look at what a garden around it would like to prepare and plan.

Sure, maybe you are not cooking with all the fresh vegetables, and that is sure. You may like flowers of different species, or you may be more concerned with ornamental plants in the yard. Do a little preparation for specific types of flower arrangements or landscaped garden areas on the theme and grow all related species for that scheme. One thing I like about starting landscape plants in my small greenhouse is the chance to mature certain plants before planting them in my landscape and then beginning another grouping of plants in the greenhouse. You can have beautiful plants in your yard and home throughout the year if you plan correctly.

Growing Vegetable

As with all plants grown in the greenhouse, making sure you do not allow the plants to overheat or dry out due to lack of water is very necessary. Most greenhouses can be temperature-controlled, but if yours is not, make sure there is enough ventilation and daily watering. Consider purchasing a covering over the roof for greenhouses located in an east-west dimension. You can find that your greenhouse gets dirty over time. This will enable the quality, so consider once a year wiping off the glass or plastic.

This section is a relaxed but insightful introduction to people looking to start growing vegetables that are quite new to gardening. It provides beginners with step-by-step instructions that direct the reader by choosing a suitable growing space for plant selection. It also offers some general and specific tips for growing vegetables and highlights some of its advantages in saving money and enhancing relaxation.

You now know what vegetables you want to grow to buy some seeds. There are many places from garden centers to newsagents that stock themes everywhere. Typical seeds of vegetables are quite small, typically less than 2–3 pounds. The number of seeds in a packet, however, varies significantly depending on the crop type. A packet of carrot seeds, for example, may contain about 100 seeds, while a packet of bean seeds may contain only about 20. Normally, this difference is proportional to the germination rate of the crop, with far fewer carrot seeds germinating than bean seeds.

The next step is to plant them once you have the seeds you want to grow. This is typically the process's most labor-intensive component. Many seed packets will have basic instructions to plant, sustain, and harvest the crop that you plan to produce. If you do not have any directions to hand, there is plenty of helpful information on the Internet, and your local library is a good resource as well. There are many different types and growing vegetable needs and difficulties associated with each of them could fill many books, so the rest of this section will concentrate on general growing tips rather than discussing all of these.

The soil in which it is grown is one of the most fundamental elements of the growth of a plant in its climate. Identifying your form of soil and making sure it is compatible with your plants can make a real difference to your production. Nevertheless, your soil type is not completely set, adding some fertilizer from a garden center will alter its properties and make a significant difference in plant health. It is important to keep a close eye on the vegetable feed that you plan to eat, it may not be as good what you put on the roses when you eat! For plants with fruits, several different organic feeds are very fine. An interesting experiment is buying a few and trying them out to see the differences in performance on a few of the same plants.

Certain animals are eating them before you make one of the greatest difficulties with growing vegetables. Planting or growing your vegetables in a greenhouse in your home. It is possible to grow vegetables in your house, particularly if you have a conservatory, and it can be a nice project for young kids. The dirt and dead leaves, however, eventually make their way into the furniture, and most people are prevented from doing this on any scale throughout the home. Greenhouses are an excellent alternative to shielding your plants from virtually any disease, but they are costly and not always a viable solution.

The Benefits of Growing Vegetables in Greenhouses

Greenhouses give many distinct advantages to individuals who grow crops for personal consumption and those who sell their crops. Whether you grow vegetables for profit or just enjoy caring for a garden as a hobby, putting your garden indoors will make it worth your effort.

In greenhouses, vegetables need the same conditions as they would face outdoors during their growing season. When gardening indoors, they should replicate as closely as possible whatever temperature, amount of water, and amount of light they would receive. The distinct advantage of doing so is the ability to provide plants with the conditions they need to thrive consistently. Outdoor plants must persevere with bad weather spells and infestations of insects. The findings are often superior because indoor plants are always in an ideal environment.

Although greenhouses can be useful throughout the winter to keep plants safe, they are also of great use in the summer. Since environmental conditions are similar to being optimal for plants, you will not have to spend as much on your garden's upkeep and repair. Nevertheless, as temperatures drop, the high energy costs associated with the operation of an indoor garden cause some growers to abandon their crops completely. If where you are living the winter is particularly cold and harsh, make sure you understand the amount of energy needed to keep your plants safe and healthy.

Consistency is the main aspect of managing a garden. If you can ensure that your plants receive daily light and water, you will be rewarded with a good crop. Forgetting to water the plants may make the crop worse and may have devastating effects. Even if the weather is too hot or cold for your crops, always keep a thermometer ready to measure the temperature and take any necessary actions.

Whether you are new to greenhouses and plan to build one from scratch or you are a professional gardener who wants to look after your flowers and vegetables better, take the time to look after your plants, and you will be amazed at the results. Different types of plants require different water quantities and light, and you may want to consider planting indigenous species in your field. While the opportunity to grow exotic plants and vegetables in a greenhouse may be enticing, if you plant those that already thrive in your field, you may be more pleased with the results. Gardening is a great pastime, and it will encourage you to enjoy your hobby as never before.

Conclusion

Gardening is one of the calmest and most calming hobbies. Most people work in their gardens and flowerbeds for hours. The greenhouse is one of the easiest ways to enjoy gardening. You will deal with your plants throughout the year with a greenhouse. Read about home greenhouses and how in your gardening you can get the most from them.

There are different kinds of greenhouses available for your home. A greenhouse kit is available. If you just start in your greenhouse hobby, this is a good way to go. These are also available online. You will be able to build your own greenhouse and learn all about home greenhouses with these kits. You can get a pack for it, no matter what size you choose.

Greenhouses come in many sizes and forms. Each is unique in its own way and is suitable for the kind of plants you wish to grow. There are those designed for beginners and those made for the professional gardener. Whatever you choose will decide what you plan to grow and how you use a greenhouse will ultimately determine your buying.

Which will you need in your backyard for a greenhouse? It will rely on what you expect to expand and how much you are prepared to spend. You get some very cheap greenhouse kits while you also have a greenhouse installed to your specifications and pay for it a little more.

Where should you start learning everything about home greenhouses? The first place to look is on the Internet. There are many websites dedicated to greenhouse planting, while some are specialized in greenhouses. This way, you will find plenty of details or visit a kindergarten that sells greenhouses.

If you choose one, you will want a robust greenhouse. You certainly do not want it to fly through the yard with high winds in the first storm.

Make sure you select a reputable dealer and search in your greenhouse for some standard construction designs.

Make sure the greenhouse you choose has a lot of ventilation windows and is made long-lasting. You can usually choose models that are more inexpensive manually, or you can choose models that move up and down like house windows. All ventilation windows must have screens to avoid insects attacking you and your plants during the warmer months.

There is a lot to learn about home greenhouses, and you will learn much when you work in one. The fun of a greenhouse is to experiment and learn what you can and cannot grow.

Construct your greenhouse early in the spring so you are ready to plant early on. Remember that with a greenhouse, you can plant your crops earlier than usual because of the warmth it will create. If living in a region with below-freezing temperatures, obviously you will not be able to plant so long as the ground is still frozen. Setting up your greenhouse may help the ground below your greenhouse thaw quicker than it otherwise would. Also, if you do intend to set up a table or other platform and put plants on top of it, waiting for the ground to thaw is not such a concern.

At the end of the growing season, you are now in a position to easily deconstruct your greenhouse. On the other hand, some people build this type of greenhouse but then decide for a variety of reasons to leave the greenhouse up. If you do this, I still recommend you remove the plastic greenhouse sheeting.

How long will your plastic sheeting last? If it is quality sheeting, and it has not been damaged during the growing season, there is no reason you could not get 3 years or more of use out of it. For this to happen, you should carefully remove it at the end of each growing season. Carefully remove the screws, staples, wires, or whatever you used to fasten the sheeting, and then gingerly roll it up. Before reinstalling the sheeting before the next growing season, wash the sheeting with soap and warm water to remove dirt, dead bugs, and the like, so that it will be clear enough to let sufficient light through.

Your total costs in constructing your greenhouse will be determined based on how big/long you decide to make your greenhouse. I would expect for a typical one you might construct in your urban/suburban back yard, you can do so for less than $200. This money will be quickly offset when you start picking produce in your backyard instead of buying it at the supermarket.

Some people do something else with a small portable greenhouse. They use it only as a starter of sorts. Let us say for example they want to grow tomatoes. Maybe they normally plant them at the beginning of June but they would like to plant them early. They plant them on May 1st and immediately cover them with a small PVC greenhouse like the one mentioned here. Then around June 1st or June 15th when the weather is much warmer and the sun is blazing hot, they remove the greenhouse. They only needed the greenhouse to extend the growing season at the beginning of the season.

Greenhouses do not have to be expensive or permanent. For a small investment, most people can fairly easily construct a portable greenhouse that will extend their growing season and that can easily be removed at the end of the growing season if you so choose.